LAKE ERIE
MURDER & MAYHEM

WENDY KOILE

THE
History
PRESS

Published by The History Press
Charleston, SC
www.historypress.com

Front cover, top left: Courtesy of the Ohio History Connection, Ohio Department of Rehabilitation and Corrections Collection; *top center*: courtesy of the National Archives, Department of Justice, Bureau of Prisons. U.S. Penitentiary, Leavenworth; *top right*: courtesy of the Ohio History Connection, Ohio Department of Rehabilitation and Corrections Collection; *bottom*: courtesy of the Bowling Green State University Library, Historical Collections of the Great Lakes.
Back cover: author's collection.

First published 2021

Manufactured in the United States

ISBN 9781467145398

Library of Congress Control Number: 2021941087

ACKNOWLEDGEMENTS

First, I would like to thank my commissioning editor, John Rodrigue, at The History Press. Your patience, feedback and encouragement carried me through the entire project. I would also like to thank the rest of the team at THP for creating a book that I am proud to share.

Also, thank you to the many librarians, curators and research coordinators for your assistance on this project, especially during the pandemic. My sincere appreciation on this project goes to Mark Peter Sprang, Bob Frisebee, Julie Mayle, Carrie Wimer, Janine Mozee, Karen Richardson and Jenni Salamon. Your expertise is invaluable.

A special thanks to my best writing friend, Jane Ann Turzillo, always there to support me. My writing friends Pam Kirst, Larissa Harper and Tracey Porter—your friendship and encouragement has got me through.

Lastly, a very special thanks to my daughter Emma Koile for her relentless support. My mom for her love, my sister, Amanda, for her expert knowledge and my Aunt Kathy for her listening ear.

Also, thank you to Matt Milhoan for your extraordinary belief in me.

Introduction

A HISTORY OF VIOLENCE

*Deep into that darkness peering, long I stood there, wondering, fearing, doubting,
dreaming dreams no mortal ever dared to dream before.*
—Edgar Allan Poe

O n an early summer day in June 1911, parents soaked up the sun
while watching their children play along the Lake Erie shoreline.
Although the water was still chilly, the youngsters could not resist
dipping their toes into the water and attempting to outrun the breakers.
When they tired of this, they resorted to another beloved activity. Carefully
selecting stones based on splash potential or skipping possibility, they gleefully
tossed handfuls of pebbles into the lake, only to scoop up more before the
first batch had hit bottom.

On that same afternoon and several miles offshore, members of the
Buffalo Police Department tossed armfuls of objects overboard the patrol
ship SS *Grover Cleveland*. Unlike the children, however, the officers carefully
observed as each item slowly twirled its way toward the bottom. Considering
that they were discarding nearly twelve hundred confiscated weapons,
including revolvers, rifles, shotguns, stilettoes, knives and dirks, the crew
made absolutely certain that their cargo disappeared into the depths.

According to the *Buffalo Enquirer* in an article published after the disposal
mission: "Many of the weapons resting on the bottom of historic Lake Erie
were identified with murder committed in the city. Others were used by
men and women, tired of the battle of life. The majority of the revolvers

117. BATH HOUSE, BOARDWALK AND BEACH, CEDAR POINT, OHIO.

A beach scene near Cedar Point. *Courtesy of the Columbus Metropolitan Library Ohio Postcard Collections.*

destroyed were taken from foreigners, who were not entitled to carry a weapon….Non-union strikers secured weapons to protect themselves from being assaulted by strikers."

For the most part, throughout its history Lake Erie has been viewed as a peaceful and enjoyable asset to the nation. Not only is it physically beautiful, but it also has offered an abundance of resources including fishing, shipping and vacationing. Yet, during its relatively quiet existence, several events hinted at a deeper, darker undertow within the 240-mile stretch of water. Just as the lake lent itself nicely for the Buffalo Police to discard items associated with evil misdeeds, it also has provided an ideal place to commit such crimes.

The first recorded acts of violence on or near the lake occurred in the 1650s. According to Eriereader.com, the Erie Indian Nation was involved in a series of conflicts with neighboring nations that included kidnappings, murders and revenge killings. Eventually, three of the tribes united with the Iroquois Confederacy and launched a targeted war against the Erie people, who occupied the areas along the Ohio, Pennsylvania and western New York shoreline. In this act to end violence with violence, the Erie people became a lost nation, with the few survivors merging with nearby tribes.

Near the end of the same century, French explorer and trader René-Robert Cavelier, Sieur La Salle launched *Le Griffon*, one of the first ships to set sail in the Great Lakes region. Embarking on August 7, 1679, from the Niagara River and landing on an island in Lake Michigan, Le Salle traded for fur from the local islanders. From there, he sent the ship with a crew of six back to Niagara while he stayed to survey the region. On September 18, the *Le Griffon* left its island port and was never seen again. Theories then, and still today, point to a violent end for the vessel and crew. Many believed that the islanders ran the ship aground, while some thought the Ottawa Indians murdered the crew and burned the vessel. La Salle himself believed that the crew deliberately sank the ship and left with the valuable cargo. Still others believed that *Le Griffon* met with a Great Lake storm and sank to the bottom, like thousands of other ships in centuries to come.

Nearly one hundred years later and after two wars concerning land rights, the Northwest Ordinance was signed into effect in 1787, allowing for the territories in the Great Lakes region to apply for statehood. Further, the ordinance guaranteed fee simple ownership of land in the area. With this in place, there was a rapid onslaught of settlers into the new Northwest. Yet just when it seemed that everything was falling into place, another violent storm was brewing just offshore of the newly settled lands.

An unidentified stranded ship on a beach near Ashtabula, Ohio. *Courtesy of Ashtabula Maritime Surface Transportation Museum.*

INTRODUCTION

In 1812, the United States declared war once again on Britain and its allies due to trade acts. This time, however, the war was fought on the water as opposed to the land. From the onset, the British navy took control over Lake Erie as a strategic move to infiltrate the United States from Canada. This eventually led to the U.S. Navy constructing forts in several harbor areas on Lake Erie in hopes of conquering the British. On September 10, 1813, the moment finally came, and a full-out battle occurred near Put-in-Bay. For hours, the blasts of cannons could be heard for miles around the lake. In the end, Oliver Hazard Perry and his men captured six British vessels. The Battle of Lake Erie, although necessary for American independence, was yet another deadly event on the small body of water. Christopher Klein of the History Channel writes of the violence aboard the warring ships.

> *The ships pounded each other round after round. Riflemen in the rigging fired at enemy brigs. Lake Erie's placid waters roiled like an ocean in a tempest. Sailors struggled to sidestep the corpses strewn on the deck, and overwhelmed surgeons could not keep up with the wounded. The captain and first lieutenant of every British vessel were killed or wounded. Barclay was taken below deck after his remaining arm was severely hurt, and after more than two hours of a brutal beating, USS* Lawrence *was reduced to a crippled hulk. Every gun facing the enemy had been disabled, and nearly all her crew were killed or wounded.*

For the next few decades, it seemed that the official warring was over. The settlers could finally concentrate on actually settling. With the advancements made during the Industrial Revolution and the natural geographic features, many settlers in the newly formed Great Lakes states found themselves in a prosperous position. The shipping industry and railroads provided lucrative work for those in proximity to the lakes. It seemed that business was booming in the former Northwest Territory, even when civil unrest began to infiltrate the states.

In 1861, the country was at war once again, but this time with itself. While the Civil War raged, the Union army realized that it needed secluded areas to send Confederate prisoners. Johnson's Island in Sandusky Bay presented not only an isolated spot, but it also was protected naturally from enemy ambush and potential escapes. For the next few years, nearly nine thousand captured, homesick soldiers rotated through the prison surrounded by the waters of Lake Erie. Today, two hundred graves on the tiny island attest to the suffering that occurred there.

Near the turn of the twentieth century, business along the lake returned to a full swing. Minus the deadly storms and a few wayward souls out on the lake, it seemed that Lake Erie was becoming a superstar of both industry and tourism. Whatever darkness had plagued the waters in the previous two and a half centuries seemed a relic of the past as people flocked to the lake to conduct business as well as relax on the sandy beaches and breezy islands. During this gilded era along the shores, it was impossible to predict that in just a few short years, the lake would become a hotbed of criminal activity.

Between 1920 and 1933, the American government banned the sale, transportation and consumption of alcohol. While this may have deterred some Americans from having access to alcohol, it led to the beginnings of organized crime, as smuggling operations formed all around the Great Lakes. Hundreds of vessels were caught zipping to and from nearby Prohibition-free Canada. Violent shoot-outs, boat wrecks and gangster-related murders ensued. Once again, Lake Erie provided easy access for such illicit activities. Unfortunately, even after the rum-running ceased when Prohibition ended, problems for the smallest of the inland seas were just getting started.

By the 1950s, Lake Erie was a huge hub of commercial activity, as the lake supplied a connection to the entire world via the water, especially after the construction of the Saint Lawrence Seaway. The problems occurred

A night scene on Lake Erie. *Courtesy of the Columbus Metropolitan Library Ohio Postcard Collections.*

when manufacturing companies located along the lake discovered a simple and cost-effective way to rid their factories of waste materials. They simply dumped waste and other unwanted chemicals directly into the lake and rivers flowing toward it. The manufacturing companies were not alone in their actions; heavily populated cities needed easy outlets for their raw sewage. As a result, the water became toxic, killing off most of the wildlife and making it unsafe for leisure use. Consequently, the lake that once was a treasured asset to the country was declared a "dead lake" in 1970.

Luckily, the declaration was the wake-up call needed for the entire country to grasp the dire condition at hand. In 1975, the Lake Erie Commission was formed to protect wildlife in and along the lake. Two years later, the Clean Water Act was implemented, regulating factory and city dumping. With new laws in place and the actions of concerned citizens, the lake slowly returned to a healthy, sustainable state over the next few decades.

As Lake Erie continues to grow, especially as a fishing and vacationing mecca, families return each year to enjoy the picturesque scenery. It is difficult to fathom that such a place was once the backdrop of bloody wars, mobster hideouts, murders and unlimited dumping. But sometimes, when the wind howls across a raging Erie sea, it blows in a hint of something more sinister. It is in these moments that one can begin to comprehend how such a lovely area just might be an ideal setting for murder and mayhem.

1

THE *SEEANDBEE*

WHEN THE LIGHTS OF CLEVELAND DISAPPEARED

When the passenger slipped to the upper decks of the cruise ship sometime in the early hours before dawn, no one noticed. The next afternoon, when the ship docked in its destined port and one passenger never disembarked, the crew did not lift an eyebrow. And when her cabin sat empty, minus her luggage, for almost two weeks, still no one sounded an alarm. In fact, it seemed that nobody on board the luxury liner had any information concerning the mysterious disappearance and death of Narene Mozee of cabin 419.

The *Seeandbee*, a play on the first letters of Cleveland and Buffalo, was one of the most luxurious cruise ships to sail the Great Lakes. With its four massive decks and a hulk measuring five hundred feet long, the *Seeandbee* easily accommodated a ballroom, several restaurants, saloons and nearly one hundred staterooms. Routine sailings, starting at Chicago, included stops at Detroit, Mackinaw Island and Cleveland's Ninth Street Pier to pick up passengers. From Cleveland, the ship sailed throughout the night to Buffalo. It was one of the few Great Lakes cruise ships to offer overnight accommodations. From Buffalo, travelers could book passage back to Ohio, Michigan or Illinois on what was called the Merry-Go-Round Tour.

In the 1940 season, *Seeandbee* marketing was meticulously targeted toward the business-class passenger. It made sense, then, that one passenger, fifty-year-old Narene Mozee, a highly skilled nurse and wife of a U.S Marshal, would choose the ship as her mode of transportation that hot July.

A 1930s brochure advertising the various ports-of-call on the *Seeandbee* tour. *Courtesy of the Bowling Green State University Library, Historical Collections of the Great Lakes.*

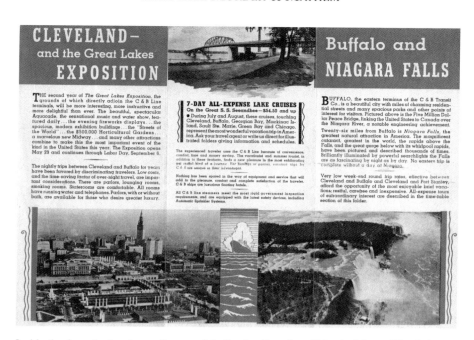

Inside the *Seeandbee* brochure. *Courtesy of the Bowling Green State University Library, Historical Collections of the Great Lakes.*

The *Seeandbee* approaching port. *Courtesy of the Bowling Green State University Library, Historical Collections of the Great Lakes.*

Narene, a native of Alaska, arrived in Cleveland a few days prior to her cruise. The plan was for Narene to visit her brother and his family there, cruise to Buffalo and then take a train to Connecticut to visit her sister. If there was time, she would possibly visit Bellevue Hospital in New York and inquire about nurses' training seminars. By all accounts, Narene had been looking forward to this adventure for the previous few weeks. And with the first, and most difficult, leg of her journey—from Alaska to the mainland—complete, the second half seemed to be a relatively simple and relaxing process. On July 29, when she boarded the opulent *Seeandbee* for an overnight voyage to Buffalo, she felt as tranquil as the greenish-blue inland sea in the backdrop.

The *Seeandbee* had docked in Cleveland unusually late that evening, postponing departure to Buffalo from 9:30 p.m. until 11:15 p.m. However, with festivities on the ship in full swing at that time of night, most passengers seemed not to mind the late departure. Narene, after checking into her cabin, found herself drawn to one of the music and dance shows atop the ship. After she returned to her room and found it unbearably hot, especially for an Alaskan, she returned to the top deck, as she stated in a letter she wrote that evening. Sometime between 1:00 a.m. and 3:00 a.m., Narene slipped quietly out of her room to make her way to the cooler upper deck.

On the morning of July 30, the *Seeandbee*, after a supposed incident-free voyage, docked at Buffalo. Among the hustle and bustle of the disembarkment process, it went unnoticed that one passenger was unaccounted for. Even more troublesome, when the ship left loaded with passengers heading west, it went undetected that a cabin was left vacant, minus the luggage of the previous passenger, a letter on the desk and an outfit carefully laid out on the bed, where it would remain untouched and unacknowledged for the next fourteen days.

For agents with the Federal Bureau of Investigation assigned to the case, things seemed backward from the start. First, on August 13, they received a call from the Cleveland Police Department that a woman had been reported missing from a steamer traversing Lake Erie. Oddly, she had been unaccounted for since July 30, two weeks prior to the report of her disappearance. Because of the suspicious circumstance, the FBI was contacted, as the possibility of a "crime on the high seas" fell under the bureau's responsibility.

Within a few hours of the first call, a second message was received via telegraph to Cleveland's FBI office. Coroner Charles Webster of Geneva, Ohio, reported to the Cleveland Police Department that he had handled

One of many dining areas aboard the *Seeandbee*. *Courtesy of the Bowling Green State University Library, Historical Collections of the Great Lakes.*

the autopsy and the burial of an unknown woman who had washed ashore at Geneva-on-the Lake on July 31. The coroner stated that the descriptions of the missing passenger and the unknown body matched. After receiving a picture of the missing woman, the coroner ascertained that the body was that of Narene Mozee, the missing passenger.

The case quickly moved from one of a suspicious disappearance to one of a suspicious death. Agents needed to strategically delegate the work at hand among the team in order to handle the myriad details associated with the case.

First was the question of the delayed reporting by the crew of the *Seeandbee*. For two weeks, the ship had continued routine cruises while cabin 419 apparently was never booked throughout that time. The question was obvious. How had the abandoned room gone unnoticed throughout the course of several voyages?

According to Captain Starchan, master of the steamer, who had filed the report on the missing passenger, he had only recently been informed of

Above: One of many sitting areas on the upper decks. *Courtesy of the Bowling Green State University Library, Historical Collections of the Great Lakes.*

Opposite: Writing and card-playing area, possibly where Narene Mozee wrote her last letter. *Courtesy of the Bowling Green State University Library, Historical Collections of the Great Lakes.*

the deserted cabin. After he spoke to his crew, it was determined that the maid supervisor had been made aware of the situation shortly after leaving Buffalo on July 31. With one hundred rooms to inspect and dozens of maids to supervise, the head maid brushed the situation to the side. During later questioning by FBI agents, she attempted to justify this by explaining that people often booked a room on the ship but did not always sleep in their cabin. She also stated that she later became alarmed when the attending maid of cabin 419 reported that the same outfit had remained on the bed for those two weeks. This is when she asked to speak to the captain.

Agents also questioned the purser's office, which handled bookings for the ship. Investigators were curious as to how Narene's cabin would not have been rebooked for the subsequent cruises. According to the purser's office, the cabin was rebooked after Narene's cruise ended. However, the maids and bellhops would not have an official manifest of guest and room assignments. Interestingly, one maid reported that a guest did attempt to check in to cabin 419 but was simply moved to another cabin after finding the luggage and clothes.

With initial questioning underway, a team of agents was assigned to secure the crime scene. On searching the cabin, agents produced two vitally

A typical business-class stateroom. *Courtesy of the Bowling Green State University Library, Historical Collections of the Great Lakes.*

important leads. First was a letter written by Narene to her son Elliot, dated July 30. The letter stated that she was writing from an outdoor upper deck of the *Seenandbee*, as her cabin was extremely warm. Narene also noted that she had watched as the "lights of Cleveland disappeared." This helped agents piece together a timeline of her movements that evening.

Second, the cabin search allowed the agents to take inventory of Narene's personal effects left in the cabin. Most important, they were able to detail what was not in the cabin. The officers reported that there was no trace of the jewelry, in particular her diamond wedding ring, or the large amount of cash that Narene had brought with her. The items had not been found with her body in Geneva. It was probable, then, that robbery was a motive in this case.

Speaking in detail to Narene's family, including her husband, U.S. Marshal Benjamin Mozee; her brother in Cleveland; her sister in Connecticut; her doctor in Nome; and several acquaintances, agents were able to garner more information. By all accounts, Narene was thrilled to be on the voyage. She was a seasoned traveler and enjoyed the water, often sailing by boat from

Alaska to Seattle. She was usually of good cheer, enjoyed her job as a nurse and easily made friends. Her hometown doctor mentioned that she had recently begun the "change of life," menopause, but seemed to be handling it well. When questioned about their marriage, Ben Mozee reported that it was a happy one. This was attested to by Narene's family and friends. Consequently, early in the case, the possibly of Narene committing suicide was ruled out.

With the newfound information and theories, agents began the daunting task of locating possible witnesses and interviewing the crew of the ship to determine if a crime had, indeed, occurred. Meanwhile, on land, agents rushed to glean information from the Geneva coroner's office on both the retrieval and autopsy of Narene's body.

According to the reports, on the evening on July 31, around 6:00 p.m, a call was received by local authorities concerning a body that had washed ashore at Lake Forest Beach, in the resort area of Geneva-on-the-Lake, Ohio. Three vacationers had noticed something floating close to the shore. When they realized that it was a human, the two gentlemen of the group waded into the water to pull the body to shore. Immediately, someone was sent to the nearby Bonnieview Cottages to call for help. Once the call was made, the owner of the cottages ran to the beach to see if it was perhaps one of her guests and then placed a blanket over the lifeless form until authorities appeared. By the time the coroner arrived on scene, nearly one hundred people had crowded the small strip of beach.

Coronor Webster stated that, on his arrival, he quickly noted the exterior condition of the body, including a swollen and black right eye. While still on the scene, the coroner inquired of the crowd as to whether any items such as jewelry or other personal belongings had been removed from the body. Notably, the group that found the body stated that it would not have been possible for anyone to remove any item without being detected, as a crowd had immediately formed at a respectable distance at the scene following the retrieval. Webster proceeded to prepare the body for transport to his lab over the next hour.

During the formal autopsy, Webster fully examined the blackened eye area, making note that it only could have occurred before death. He also included in the report that, in his opinion, there was "some evidence of violence in this case" and "fingers of both hands were spotted more or less like leopard spots with something that looked like tar." Finally, Webster noted that Narene Mozee seemed to be in overall good health, with no signs of disease or sickness. Her final cause of death was listed as drowning.

After reviewing information provided by the coroner and local authorities, the federal investigators moved to have the body exhumed from Ashtabula County and sent to their Cleveland lab for a more thorough autopsy. One week after burial, the body was exhumed from the unmarked grave and transported one hour away to the city.

Back on the *Seeandbee*, investigators continued to gather evidence, including a list of all passengers on board, room locations, crew and their positions and reports from potential witnesses on the ship during Narene's cruise. Churning through the information, agents sought additional information from several people who they thought potentially could provide pertinent clues.

The first was a passenger by the name of Goethe Faust, a lawyer from Pennsylvania. Faust, a first-time cruiser assigned to cabin 421, was accompanied by a boyhood friend, a Mr. Miller from Cleveland. After the ship left dock at approximately 11:15 p.m., the two made their way to a popular taproom on the top deck known as the Rathskeller. Here they met "a girl in a green dress" who would later be identified as Dorthey Perry.

Conflicting stories between Faust and Perry emerged during questioning. Faust stated that Perry invited him to see her room, cabin 431, and then asked him to wait while she went to the ladies' room. She stated that she had slipped on stairs, causing a delay in her return. Faust stated that, while waiting in the room, he became tired and stretched out on her bed. When Perry returned, Faust claimed that he left the room without incident. On the other hand, Perry said that Faust invited himself into the room, having "other ideas in mind." She then told him to leave, which he did. When Faust returned to his own room around 2:30 a.m., he found Miller asleep on his bed. After arguing with Miller to go to his own room, Faust gave up and decided to put on his pajamas and sleep on the sun deck.

Authorities' interest was piqued, as both Perry and especially Faust could have possibly came into contact with Narene as she went on deck to write her letter. However, under extensive questioning, both Perry and Faust insisted that they had not noticed a woman matching Narene's description.

A second person sought for heavy questioning was a night watchman named Robert Smalley. Initially, detectives were satisfied with the watchman's report. However, when they learned that Smalley quit his job on August 13 after two years of employment with the Cleveland and Buffalo Transit Company, they decided to take a closer look.

Smalley's job was to make rounds every twenty minutes from 10:00 p.m. to 6:00 a.m. His rounds required that he patrol the upper decks, punching a key card at the completion of each round. During his first interview, Smalley stated that he did not see Narene on the deck or coming or going from her room, although he passed by her cabin several times on his nightly rounds. He also stated that he did not remember seeing anyone on deck after 1:00 a.m. but retracted the statement when pressed during a second interview. Smalley confessed that he remembered seeing a woman in her nightgown who had slipped and broken her shoe. Later, authorities realized that he was describing Dorthey Perry.

Smalley told investigators that he quit his job on the *Seeandbee* due to the long and physically demanding hours required. On further investigation, agents learned that Smalley suffered from several health conditions that required back surgery at one point. Satisfied overall with Smalley, who remained forthcoming throughout the questionings, investigators turned their eyes to one last lead.

In most murder cases involving a married person, the spouse is the first to be questioned as a suspect. But in this case, with the husband nearly four thousand miles away at the time of the disappearance and with his respected position as a U.S. Marshall, Ben Mozee was one of the last to be questioned as a potential suspect.

The first line of business, then, was to take a closer look at the Mozees' marriage. In correspondence between investigating agencies, it was noted that although Marshal Mozee "had been very cooperative with the Bureau and has done everything to assist the Bureau…it is felt advisable for the Bureau office to make a discreet investigation at Nome to determine the condition of Mrs. Mozee's home life and her general temperament."

Apparently, Ben had been married once before. From his first marriage, he had two children and custody of the pair. The children lived with Ben and Narene, who also had a son during their own marriage. Digging deep into the family relationship, agents learned that the Mozees seemed to have a stable, happy relationship. Likewise, Narene appeared content to have her stepchildren in the home. Ben told investigators that he and his wife did have normal disagreements, as all couples do.

After friends and family concurred with Ben's opinion of the marriage and home life, investigators took a look at a second possible motive. Learning that the Mozees had taken out a traveler's insurance policy for Narene, Ben being the beneficiary of the $5,000, agents made a visit to Traveler's Insurance Company in Seattle, Washington. Here they learned that the policy filed by Ben on July, 10, 1940, covered up to thirty days of travel. However, the policy covered only accidental injury and death. Specifically,

Narene and Ben Mozee and their children. *Courtesy of the Mozee family archives.*

the policy denied the release of funds in the event of Narene's suicide or murder. Notably, Ben had insisted from the start that Narene's death was an act of foul play, forgoing any chance at receiving the insurance money.

Meanwhile, the second autopsy report was finalized. Most telling, the coroner found that Narene had chemicals, grease, on her hands and under her nails that matched the materials found on the sun deck or top deck of the ship. Second, the coroner stated that the blunt force trauma to the head had most likely occurred an hour or so before death. The new evidence suggested a violent struggle atop the ship, with Narene possibly grabbing the ship railing and ropes in an attempt to stop herself from going overboard.

With no official persons of interest, FBI agents began to wrap up the investigation. After thoroughly questioning over two hundred people who had been onboard the night of Narene's death, including crew and guests, and probing into Narene's personal life, the case quietly went cold.

As the months wore on, Narene's family came to realize that the case would possibly never be solved. Doors seemed to close one by one, starting with a failed lawsuit by Ben Mozee against the Cleveland and Buffalo Transit Company. Later that year, the *Seeandbee*—along with its secret—was sold to the U.S. military. The ship was converted to a military aircraft carrier, the

Wolverine, serving throughout World War II. It was salvaged for scrap in 1947. Finally, John Edgar Hoover, director of the Federal Bureau of Investigation, deemed the Mozee case completed. In his letter to the Director of Marine Inspection and Navigation, Hoover stated that "a complete inquiry was conducted by representatives" and that "the information secured during the course of the investigation failed to disclose that the death of Mrs. Mozee was due to anything other than accidental causes."

The questions concerning Narene's mysterious death will most likely never be answered, leaving the details to fade away, much as the light of Cleveland did on that fateful night.

2

THE ASHTABULA BANK HEIST

IF YOU ARE GOING TO BE A BANDIT

On a stifling July evening in 1921, phase one of the heist was underway. As "Slim" awaited the arrival of the getaway transportation, he reviewed the plan that had been in the works for several weeks. The blueprints for the job were so brilliant that he could practically write a book, or at least tell the details to newspaper reporters, in the event of his capture.

It was just a matter of some diligent planning, really. First, to execute a successful heist, one must choose a bank wisely. One positioned along a huge body of water would work splendidly, as the employees were accustomed to unknown men from the docking ships patronizing the place. So bank officials would not question a new customer and allow unhindered access to the teller counters. Second, one had to coordinate the getaway. Here again, the lakefront location lent itself nicely to the plan, offering a watery escape route that an amateur robber would miss altogether. Hence, a stolen, fully stocked yacht would be ideal for smooth water travel. Third, one had to remember to work with guns blazing. One had to fire off warning shots throughout the job to establish authority, even if no one was shooting back. And last, and possibly most important, a robber had to be certain that everyone in the operation had a gangster-like alias. Not only would this prevent a witness from overhearing one's real name, but pseudonyms would also alert the authorities that they were dealing with professionals.

For Slim and his boys, the skillful planning had begun in Cleveland one early summer day in June. "Shotgun Larry," later considered the brains of the operation, devised the supposedly foolproof plan that targeted the

Ashtabula National Marine Bank. The bank, in operation since 1910, catered to the shipping crewmen and dock workers who crowded the harbor streets throughout the busy shipping seasons. Primarily, though, the bank was only yards from the waterfront, a detail on which the entire getaway hinged.

With the location set, the gang of bandits began the next steps. On the night of July 7, Slim worked his magic and "borrowed" a large car in Cleveland. Meanwhile, around 2:00 a.m. on July 8, two other bandits quietly rowed out into the Rocky River Harbor. Choices were plentiful within the yacht club, but only the best would do for the job. Spotting the most luxurious vessel, the two rowed close to the yacht and fastened a towline to it. Next, avoiding any noise or quick movements, the men tugged their new ride out into the open water of Lake Erie and started the engine for takeoff. Laughing into the night air, they jetted east toward Ashtabula, where they would soon dock their vessel.

Later that morning, at 11:30, the appointed meeting time, the four men in the vehicle drove to the wharf in Ashtabula. Like clockwork, another testament to their brilliant strategizing, the two-man crew of the stolen yacht came sailing into harbor at 11:40. By noon, all systems were go.

Easing into a parking space at the nearby barbershop, just a few feet from the bank's entrance, four of the bandits gathered up their weapons

A postcard depicting the Rocky River Harbor, where the first phase of the Ashtabula Bank heist began. *Courtesy of the Columbus Metropolitan Library Ohio Postcard Collections.*

Ashtabula National Maritime Bank. *Courtesy of Ashtabula Maritime Surface Transportation Museum.*

and nerve. With quick strides, the three men (the fourth waited in the car) entered the lobby, where they were greeted with the friendly smile of Mary Scalla.

Immediately, one man pointed a gun at Mary and demanded that she put her hands up. Thinking it was a joke, Mary laughed but was promptly told that this was no joking matter and that it was time "to shell out the money and be damned quick about it." The gunman roughly led Mary behind the teller line and instructed her to head toward the vault. While the bank robber stopped to investigate one of the teller drawers, Mary quietly slipped down the hallway and tripped the alarm, which sounded in a store about a half block away.

Meanwhile, another bandit led Achelle Martella to the vault. The robber insisted that Achelle, a bank teller, turn the combination to open the large metal door. However, the quick-thinking Achelle was not going to simply hand over the cash so hard earned by the people of his town. Instead of dialing the combination, Achelle slammed the door shut, which locked it for the next forty-eight hours.

Frustrated, the three bandits haphazardly began stuffing money from the teller drawers into their bags, forgoing an extra $15,000 in the tightly sealed vault. With sirens in the distance, they moved swiftly to the lobby and made their way to the door, where they could see the getaway car now idling in the street. Barking a few last random orders, the three made their exit.

With police cruisers now in pursuit and a car full of men careening down Harbor Street, shop owners and visitors realized that something was terribly amiss. If there were any doubts that the harbor was in trouble, they were curtailed as the sound of firing guns permeated the air. While some took cover within the shops and behind telephone poles, others, like police officer Patrick Shannon, took aim at the speeding vehicle.

Apparently, Officer Shannon, who was not on duty, had heard the bank alarm just moments earlier while attending to his own errands in town. Jumping into action, he rushed into a store where he knew a riot gun was stored. As he exited the store, he saw a car barreling down the street, at which time he opened fire. A cascade of bullets from revolvers and shotguns was returned, with one hitting Shannon in the mouth and knocking him to the ground. He later recovered from the injury.

While the car continued down the street, so did the rain of bullets, shattering storefront windows and splintering wooden walls. One oblivious bystander, Robert Grant, was working in the shoe-shinning parlor. As the window of the store exploded, a searing pain ripped through his thumb when he was struck with one of the dozens of bullets whizzing through the shop.

Bridge Street, Ashtabula, where the bandits made their getaway. *Courtesy of the Columbus Metropolitan Library Ohio Postcard Collections.*

Meanwhile, L.M. Norris, commissioner of the Lake Carriers Association for Ashtabula Harbor, took aim from his office window. Norris, too, was met with returned fire, which damaged his office building.

Just as suddenly as the commotion started, it stopped with the last rounds of fire toward Norris's office. Another police squadron arrived and was met with pedestrians cowering behind objects, a crowd forming near the bank and an officer down in the street. Either an old-fashioned gunfight had just occurred or, based on the tellers filing out of the bank, a robbery took place.

As police sought information regarding the crime, they slowly pieced together information based on eyewitness accounts. First, they garnered a physical description of the bandits and their getaway car. They also learned that the robbers had made off with an estimated $11,000 and that they were traveling east on Harbor Street. Most important, they learned that an unfamiliar boat had been noticed tied up in the harbor earlier that day but had disappeared sometime that morning. With this information, the police determined that a lake search was necessary. They also learned that a luxury yacht had been anchored off Ninevah Beach a few miles west of Ashtabula just hours before the holdup.

Within hours of the robbery, the search was underway on land, air and water, with the heaviest concentration on the lake. Throughout the afternoon and into late evening, searchers patrolled the water between Cleveland and Conneaut. With news traveling fast, numerous privately owned water vessels entered the search, while those on land scoured the highways and byways. The *Cleveland Plain Dealer* reported that a small search posse made up of farmers with rifles, pitchforks and farm implements had formed, as news spread to the countryside.

Meanwhile, more clues surfaced at police headquarters as they learned that a car as well as a yacht had been stolen from the Rocky River area shortly before the heist. The car, a Marmon, went missing Tuesday night while it was parked on Clifton Boulevard in Lakewood. Witnesses in Ashtabula matched the stolen car to the getaway car, even producing a license plate number. However, when the number was traced, they learned that the plates had been transferred from another stolen car, which had been swiped on June 7 from a Cleveland neighborhood.

The missing yacht was reported the same morning as the stolen Marmon. Apparently, the luxury watercraft, the *Merry G*, belonged to Howard Staley, a prominent businessman and vice-commodore of the Cleveland Yacht Club. Staley reported that not only was the boat stocked with enough gas to run for about three hundred miles, but it was also supplied with several days' worth of food and drink.

When the *Merry G*, empty of gas, was recovered on July 9 just off the village of Euclid, authorities speculated on two possibilities concerning the bandits' disappearance.

First, police considered that the robbers may have headed for Canada. Although the yacht was found closer to American land, it was possible that the watercraft was met by another boat. This would explain why the *Merry G* was out of gas; the gang had syphoned it into the second getaway vessel to make the long haul to the Canadian side.

The second possibility was that the criminals had made landfall during the night and used an automobile to return to Cleveland. If so, the gang members were most likely shacked up in the city, making them almost impossible to find. Even with the collaboration of three counties, including Cuyahoga, Lake and Ashtabula, the bandits remained at large, suggesting that this was not their first rodeo. Other than a description of the robbers who had entered the bank, police did not have much to go on.

As the warm waters of Lake Erie turned colder during the fall of 1921, so, too, did the case. That is, until a remarkedly similar bank robbery was reported in Niagara Falls, New York, just a few months later.

Reports stated that at around 12:30 p.m. on October 31, several rifle-wielding bandits entered the Niagara Falls Trust Company. In a flurry of shouting and shooting, the men ordered the tellers and customers to the rear of the counting rooms. During the frenzy, bank teller Katherine Wood was shot in the leg. When the vice-president of the bank, Felix Woolworth, attempted to stop one of the men during the holdup, the bandit took aim and fired at Woolworth's head, the bullet grazing his cheek. During the madness, Patrolman George Hollahan attempted to enter the bank. However, just as quickly as he busted through the door, one of the robbers aimed and fired, shooting the officer in the head. Stepping over the injured policeman, the gang made their exit.

Outside, a Peerless model car, later determined to have been stolen, idled in the roadway. Plowing through the doors, the bandits continued to fire, this time hitting Albert Van Auken, a bank patron who had been standing near the car, as well as Mildred Kitt, another bank teller who had fled from the scene.

Like the Ashtabula heist, as the bandits tore off, they continued to fire their guns, not caring who or what they hit along the way. Several police cruisers and locals gave chase, but they were met with a barrage of gunfire as the getaway car barreled through intersections and then toward the outskirts of town. With one last steady stream of shots at the pursuers, the Peerless car disappeared near Saunder's Settlement Road in a cloud of smoke, taking nearly $12,000 with it.

As the dust settled back in town, the aftershocks of the robbery were felt. Numerous victims were rushed to the hospital. Policeman Hollahan, barely alive, was taken straight to surgery, where surgeons searched to no avail for the bullet lodged in his head. Hollahan remained in the hospital for weeks fighting for his life, eventually recovering but with severe paralysis.

In the hours following the heist, while policemen gathered forces and interviewed witnesses, an individual reported an abandoned car on Lockport Road. The vehicle, a Peerless, contained three rifles and bags of ammunition. Police now believed the bandits had a second getaway car or had fled to the woods near Lockport Road. A massive search, with the aid of soldiers from Fort Niagara, was made of the entire rural area, but no other traces of the gang were found.

But for one detective on the case, lead detective Callinan, a cold trail was not going to deter him. Since the initial reports of the crime, something tickled the back of his mind. While reviewing the robbery reports again, he paused on the eyewitness account made by Katherine Wood. Not only did her physical description of the robber sound familiar to him, but something in the account of the man's demeanor also set the detective's senses on alert.

Acting on a hunch, Callinan obtained a photograph from the Niagara Falls rouges' gallery wall. The mugshot was that of Harlow Tower, alias "Slim," wanted for questioning in a fur coat store robbery in Buffalo. The mugshot had been taken the previous January, when Callinan had booked Tower on charges of vagrancy about a year before the robbery, although he had suspicions then that Tower had been involved in some local store robberies.

Showing the photograph to witnesses, Callinan was met with mixed responses. Some of the witnesses, like Katherine Wood, were sure that this was one of the bandits. Others could not say for certain. Even with the conflicting answers, the seasoned detective felt that he had his guy. And later that week, when it was learned that the Peerless getaway car had been stolen from Cleveland, Callinan was able to establish that Tower had connections in that city. Most interesting, the Cleveland Police Department informed the detective that a bank heist in Ashtabula three months prior was orchestrated similarly to the one that occurred at the Niagara Falls Trust Company. With this information, Callinan sought witnesses from both states as the pieces of the puzzle began to fall into place.

Slowly but surely, clues trickled in to both Cleveland and Niagara Falls Police Departments, finally resulting in a break in the case in mid-December. Apparently, someone had heard a woman in a restaurant in Cleveland mentioning a man by the name of Slim. When police questioned the woman, they learned that she was the girlfriend of August Reid, believed to have been involved in the robberies as well as a close friend of the infamous Slim. The woman, in fear of being incriminated herself, provided the names of all gang members involved in both heists, even reporting that she believed the men may be hiding out in New York City.

Quickly, Callinan and his team descended on a tenement on East Fifty-Fifth Street in New York on December 23, 1921. Inside, they found Harlow Tower and August Reid, both appearing exhausted, hungry and dirty. During the arrest, Tower, the more talkative of the two, informed the detectives that he and his associate would not be providing any information on either robbery. However, after twelve hours of questioning and learning that concrete evidence was found against them, both men signed confessions.

Over the next few days, Tower gleefully recounted the robberies to both the police and the *Buffalo Daily*. When questioned further about the Ashtabula National Marine Bank robbery, Tower stated, "That Ashtabula job was a real peacherino!" He continued to describe how both robberies were planned well in advance, with locations chosen by an advance agent. Tower stated that they "never went in for small game. If you are going to be a bandit be a real one and pick the big game." He also purported that diagrams of the bank and maps of the city were studied profusely and the escape route was physically rehearsed a few hours ahead of time. Tower likewise boasted how he had been an auto mechanic in the military, using his skills to hotwire cars on more than one occasion. The money was divided between the members, each lying low for a few weeks until the heat was off.

By early January 1922, the last of the gang was rounded up and brought to Niagara Falls to stand trial. The members included Harlow "Slim" Tower, August "Auggie" Reid, Larry "Shotgun" Hirsch, Joseph Principano, John "Red" Brenan and Patrick Toca, alias "Gospel Pat." Of the six, five had successful careers in the military, making the crimes more shocking to their family and friends. Later that month, all six men were sentenced to twenty years in Auburn Prison, a penitentiary known for its harsh treatment of inmates.

That same year, Detective Callinan was promoted to chief of detectives for his role in the capture and arrest of the bandits. According to the *National*

Police Journal, Callinan's expertise "attracted the attention of leading police executives of the nation." Likewise, he received a reward of $10,000 for his efforts, which he divided among himself and his team. Perhaps long before the robberies of 1921, Chief Detective Callinan had decided that if he was going to be a detective, he was going to be a real one.

3

THE *ATLANTIC*

A RIPPLE EFFECT

I n the depths of Lake Erie lie thousands of sunken ships. Some of those skeletons remain undiscovered and possibly lost to time. Hundreds of others have been found and explored by divers, scientists and historians. Strangely, there is one ship, the *Atlantic*, that is guarded by tens of thousands of dollars' worth of electronic sensing devices to prevent trespassing near and on the wreckage. What is it about the remains of this ship that has caused controversy between two countries since the day of its demise over a century and a half ago? Perhaps just like the sinking of it, the person or persons responsible for the lost steamer will forever be the subject of debate.

EXHAUSTION, LIKE THE MISTY, humid air, clung to them like a damp shirt. As they boarded the passenger paddlewheel steamer *Atlantic* during the late evening hours of August 19, 1852, they could barely keep their eyes open. As soon as they found a spot among the stacks of luggage, carts and other passengers, they all but collapsed on the deck. For most, this overcrowded stint from New York to Michigan by way of the Great Lakes would be just one more in a series of difficult travels. Prior to that, most of the passengers had faced extreme hardship before leaving their homeland. After traveling from Norway, Ireland and other northern European countries to Ontario and then on to Buffalo over the past two and a half months, for the passengers, the sixteen-hour trip across the Great Lakes, most of which they would sleep through, seemed the least of their worries.

European Immigrants boarding the SS *Angelo* bound for America. *Courtesy of the Library of Congress Digital Collections.*

Meanwhile, non-emigrant passengers boarded the *Atlantic* and headed straight to their first-class accommodations. It was not uncommon for an American passenger ship to take on emigrant passengers coming by way of Ontario or the East Coast, as they were arriving weekly in those days. Many were headed to the Midwest in search of promised fertile farming ground, while some were hoping to secure a job on the ever-expanding railway. What was unusual to see onboard the ship was the number of passengers, especially after the steamer stopped at Erie around 10:00 p.m. and boarded several hundred more people.

As the purser rushed around the deck, collecting passage with no rhyme, reason or records, the *Atlantic*, now completely overloaded with luggage and lives, steamed out of the Erie port at 11:00 p.m. Because this particular voyage allowed for no place to stroll or socialize, and because of the sheer exhaustion of many, it seemed that the entire body of passengers promptly fell asleep as the ship entered the calm open waters of Lake Erie. In less than a day, they would reach their destination and this sticky, foggy night would be behind them.

Sometime around 2:00 a.m., however, the peaceful silence was shattered as a cracking sound penetrated the quiet night air. The people on deck jerked awake just in time to see one of the tall mast poles crash down onto an upper deck, followed by screams of those in proximity to it. Immediately following the crash, they realized that the nose of another large ship, the *Ogdensburg*, was positioned along the starboard side, with both ships forming a capital *T*.

Those in the staterooms, both hearing and feeling the commotion, sprang from their beds and made their way to the open decks, where they saw the other large ship slowly push away as though untangling itself from the *Atlantic*.

In the next instant, it seemed as if the ships sat frozen in position. After the short hesitation, the *Ogdensburg* and *Atlantic* began to right themselves back onto their intended courses. Astonishingly, within a few minutes, both ships were on their way, as if they simply dusted themselves off and went about their business. After all, the vessels had deadlines to meet, and a few scrapes need not affect their arrival times into port.

Unfortunately, though, a little more than a scrape had occurred. As the *Atlantic* inched westward, a shutter was felt just as passengers on the port side began to flee their cabins. In the collision, the bow of the *Ogdensburg* had pierced a huge hole into the side of the *Atlantic*, allowing water to flood the lower levels of the ship.

As crew and passengers scattered about among the overstacked luggage, a full-blown panic began to set in. Words of many languages were shouted into the night, followed by the sound of items being thrown into the water. Hundreds of passengers scrambled, searching for their families as well as their belongings, as some had boarded with their remaining life's possessions. Many sought out crew members in hopes of reassurance, only to be met with panicked gestures of an untrained team. Worst of all, the sinking sensation was notable, as the ship was taking on water at an unbelievable rate.

Meanwhile, the captain of the *Ogdensburg*, now a few miles away, had directed that the ship be stopped in order to assess damage. But as the crew evaluated the vessel for potential problems, a sickening noise carried over the water from the west. To their horror, they heard the unmistakable sound of human screams. Instantly, they realized that the other ship must be in trouble. Quickly, they reversed the engines and began what seemed like the longest voyage of their lives, back to the scene of the wreck.

As the *Ogdensburg* made its way back, the crew of the *Atlantic* set to releasing the three lifeboats available. Forcefully pushing back passengers, the crew helped the captain onto the first launch. Just as he stepped over the side, the ropes slipped through the crewmates' hands, causing the captain to pitch forward. The lifeboat hit the water with a loud thud just as the captain landed on his head on the floor on the boat, causing a severe concussion that left him confused throughout the rest of the ordeal.

While the crew struggled to cut lines and untangle other lifeboats, many passengers made the decision to jump into the water. Although the water temperature was at a survivable temperature in the late-summer month, the bedlam was not. Many people could not swim. Some began to grasp onto one another in the deep water, pulling one another down. Others held on to furniture and luggage, only to have others join, overweighting the object until it was useless. For those strong swimmers who attempted to assist the strugglers, the language barrier along with the panic and noise level prevented nearby passengers from understanding. To make matters worse, the bow of the *Atlantic* began to sink below the water line, lifting a great portion on the ship up a few feet.

By this time, the *Ogdensburg* had entered the debris field, where it circled the half-submerged *Atlantic*. The *Ogdensburg* positioned itself alongside the troubled ship, and passengers who had remained on the *Atlantic* walked onto the deck of the arriving ship. The *Ogdensburg* continued to troll the area for hours in hopes of locating survivors, but most were lost to the dark waters.

By DAYBREAK, NEWS OF the tragedy had reached land, as attested to by headlines in the *Buffalo Morning Express*. The *Express* stated: "It becomes our painful duty to record one of the most fatal collisions that has ever occurred upon the Lakes—involving a dreadful loss of human life, besides the destruction of one of our first-class steamers.…The question of blame—for we do not see how such an accident could occur without blame—must be left for future consideration." Newspapers across the country carried similar reports with a focus on determining who was at fault.

Initially, it seemed that the *Atlantic* and its crew were clearly a fault. As survivors brought forth claims of the crew's incompetence, inadequate and faulty life-saving supplies and overcrowding on the ship, the Erie County prosecutor sought to bring charges against E.B Ward, owner of the *Atlantic*.

Over the next few years, debates continued regarding the collision. Both the owners of the *Atlantic* and the owners of the *Ogdensburg* held the other at fault, especially once it was determined that the wreck was due to human error and not mechanical malfunction. To make matters worse, rumors circulated that one ship could have intentionally caused the collision in hopes of damaging or destroying a rival ship. The competition to be the fastest ship was attested to by both captains' decisions to continue on course without stopping immediately following the crash.

In 1856, the U.S. Supreme Court ruled that both ships were equally responsible for the disaster. Soon after, Congress passed a law requiring ships to be licensed and thoroughly inspected before setting sail. Because no records were kept, the official number of passengers on board is not known. Based on eyewitness accounts, it is likely there were anywhere between three to four hundred passengers and crew, with over half not surviving the wreck, making it the fifth-worst disaster in Great Lake history.

MEANWHILE, A FEW MONTHS after the wreck, as the *Atlantic* settled into its final resting place a few miles off Long Point, Ontario, another pressing issue emerged. Apparently, the ship had been transporting a safe for the American Express Company containing $36,000. In October 1852, American Express hired diver John Green to retrieve the safe from the cabin. Over the next few years, Green searched for the treasure, reaching a new record-setting diving-depth level in the process. In 1855, he finally located the safe and was able to pull it to the deck of the *Atlantic*. However, during this excursion, Green suffered a nearly fatal case of the bends, or decompression sickness. After recovering, he returned to the wreck site in 1856, only to find that the safe and its contents had disappeared.

It was soon discovered that another diver, Elliot Harrington, and his team had retrieved the safe. With this information, the American Express Company brought Harrington to court. The court ruled that the safe rightly belonged to the company, but it did award Harrington and his team members almost $2,000 each for their efforts.

Over the next few years, other diving teams continued to search the wreckage for any valuables, but to no avail. Eventually, as the *Atlantic* nestled deeper into the sand and as plant life took over, the ship was all but abandoned.

It was not until nearly a century later that professional diver Michael Fletcher set out to find the *Atlantic* in the early 1980s in hopes to study and preserve the history associated with the wreck. Amazingly, the ship was quite intact and was easily found after a recent zebra mussel invasion. The mussels had eaten away much of the plant life, exposing the hulk of the ship. After several diving expeditions, Fletcher was able to retrieve the ship's bell, telegraph and hundreds of crockery items, which he sent to be preserved via regulations of the Canadian Shipping Act.

In 1991, a California-based diving company, Mar-Dive, announced that it had rediscovered the shipwreck. The company paid the state of Ohio $14,000 to re-form the Western Wrecking Company, which had searched for the ship in 1867.

With the rediscovery of the ship and the amount of interest by both professional and amateur divers, Ontario historians became concerned for the preservation of the ship after learning that the Mar-Dive Company had plans to auction recovered items.

In 1997, the courts ruled that the *Atlantic* was within Canadian waters. Ownership was granted to the Providence of Ontario, even though it was an American ship at the time of the sinking. Since it had been abandoned in the 1860s by the Ward family, the ship had sat for a century and a half without an official owner.

Today, the *Atlantic* is heavily guarded by high-tech sensors that alert Ontario's law enforcement if a vessel lingers above or near the wreck site. Inside the rusted walls still rest the trunks and suitcases of hundreds who never had a chance to claim them.

4

THE LONG POINT LIGHTHOUSE MYSTERY

Every murderer is probably somebody's old friend.
—*Agatha Christie*

L ate in December 1884, William Dickinson was quietly keeping an eye on a not-so-quiet lake. As the cold winds blew across the peninsula, the waves built into a rolling frenzy. Although it would be unusual for a ship to be out to sea or crossing the channel that late in the season, it was not unheard of, as the lake was not yet frozen. From his watchtower, William scanned the area for any signs of distress. After six years of watching over the same few miles of water and shoreline, William's eyes had trained themselves to spot anomalies. Consequently, when he noticed a dark object floating on the billowing waves near the shoreline, he knew something was amiss. Further observing the oblong shape, he determined that it was not a log, which is a typical object to see tossed about the waves, especially during high winds. Focusing his telescope on the item, he watched as it was churned over several times in the rough surf. All his instincts and experience told him that what he was looking at was a body.

The Long Point Cut Lighthouse was different from the two other lights positioned on Long Point peninsula, a sand spit extending nearly twenty-five feet into Lake Erie on the Ontario side. One lighthouse marked the tip of the peninsula, while the other guarded the west harbor. After a storm washed open a wider channel, or cut, through the peninsula, a lightship was positioned to mark the eastern entrance in 1865. As the years passed by, more ships began to use the channel as a shortcut through the long sandpit, shaving off nearly twenty-five miles around it. By 1879, the Canadian government deemed that a lighthouse was needed as the channel became more heavily traveled. Unlike most lighthouses built in response to shipwrecks, the Long Point Cut Lighthouse was built before many could occur. Instead, the beacon was mainly a navigational guide through the area as opposed to a rescue station. Although in the case of a nearly frozen body floating in December waters, any lifesaving attempts would be futile.

As William made his way to the deserted beach, he watched as the lifeless body was flung about like a ragdoll on the frothing, furious breakers. Taking a deep breath, the lightkeeper entered the nearly frozen waters in an attempt to retrieve the shell of what was once a man. Fighting the surf and hoping that he would not become immobile due to the frigid waters, William extended his arms as far as possible, finally grasping the dead man's shirt and heaving him to shore. Dropping the body away from the reach of the lake, William collapsed into the cold sand to catch his breath.

A few minutes later, as the adrenaline wore off and his breathing returned to normal, William surveyed the body. Most peculiar was that both sets of the deceased's limbs were tied. If the man had been a sailor and died at sea, as William originally suspected, why would he be tied like this? Second, William noted that half the man's face appeared to be caved inward, as if the entire side of his head had been bashed. While not a doctor or a coroner, William assessed that the wounds were probably done pre-death as opposed to being caused by his time in the water. He then searched the man's clothing for any type of identification but found no clues.

As William considered the situation, he sighed in sadness for the man whose life had been cut short, most likely in an unnatural and brutal manner. Although there was nothing to be done to save his fellow man, William wished to give peace and dignity to the man's soul. So, he set to the task of providing a proper burial later that afternoon. Dragging the body farther inward and deeper into the peninsula to protect it from the elements, William placed the unknown man into a shallow grave, cut away the ropes, said a prayer, covered it with sand and rocks and marked it with a piece of driftwood.

Later that afternoon, he contacted the Norfolk County authorities, detailing the day's events and offering a description of the body. Officials agreed to pass along the information to newspapers in hopes of someone coming forward to identify and claim the body.

Over the next few months, as William attended to his lightkeeping duties—a mundane schedule during the heart of winter—he often wondered about the person buried not far from his station. Surely, someone somewhere was missing him. And as much as he wished to put it out of his mind, the image of the man's bound limbs and smashed face continued to haunt the lightkeeper. The entire situation was not only morose, but eerie as well. Fortunately, it would not be long before some of the lightkeeper's questions were answered.

On the early morning of March 10, 1885, just as the lake began its spring thaw, Ontario detective John Wilson Murray and John Piggott of Bay City, Michigan, arrived at the Long Point Cut Lighthouse. Detective Murray explained that Piggott had been searching for his brother, Marshall Piggott, who had last been seen walking toward the lake from his Malahide home on November 17. When John Piggott read of the unknown body found near the lighthouse, forty miles from Marshall's home, he felt there could be a connection.

Slipping on his jacket, William led the way to the gravesite, which had gone undisturbed, based on the driftwood marker still in place. Here, the detective deemed it necessary to uncover the corpse, and the three began the unimaginable task of exhuming the body that had been in the ground for four months. Uncomfortableness aside, the trio pulled the still chilled sand away from the area until the decomposing body was revealed.

A quick glance at the man's face ascertained that there would be no way to identify him through facial features. Moving his eyes away from the mutilated head, John Piggott gazed over the chest area. Gingerly running his hand over the tattered coat, John felt what he feared he would. A large protrusion of the upper chest attested to his brother's condition, known as pectus carinatum. Sometimes called "pigeon chest," the rare congenital deformity is caused by an overgrowth in cartilage, causing the breastbone to protrude outward at an odd angle.

On further inspection of the body, John Piggott established that he recognized the boots that were still on the man's feet. They had been a gift from their mother. However, there was always the chance that someone else had bought the same pair of boots. To be sure that he was indeed looking at his brother, John removed the boot of the right foot. Since birth, Marshall had had a deformed toe. Once the foot of the dead man was exposed, John had no doubt that this was his brother.

Although the question of who was in the grave was now answered, how he ended up there was not. When Detective Murray, Ontario's first official detective, learned that the man's limbs had been tied and his face smashed, his suspicions kicked into gear. As the detective and John Piggott transported Marshall's remains to Elgin County, Murray began a preliminary investigation, questioning John about his brother's life and last known activities.

Marshall Piggott, age thirty-five at time of his death, was a farmer near the lakeshore, about forty miles west of Long Point. Marshall had inherited the fifty-acre farm from his father. In 1881, Marshall had married Sarah Beauchamp, and the couple welcomed a baby boy, Marshall Francis, in 1883. Marshall and John's mother lived nearby the farm and frequently visited Marshall and his family, and vice versa. From the outside looking in, all seemed well on the Piggott farm.

However, as Murray learned more about Marshall, another layer of his life, one laced with sadness, emerged. During his life, Marshall had been teased for his physical deformity and slow speech. To make matters worse, while Marshall was by all accounts a happy-go-lucky man, he was considered to be "simple and of slow mind." Because of this, he had been taken advantage of on numerous occasions. His kindness, combined with a blind trust, often led to problems for the farmer. When Marshall wed Sarah, the family was somewhat relieved, as it seemed that she kept a close eye on those types of situations. Unfortunately, the security and happiness of the marriage lasted only a few years. Sarah died shortly after giving birth to their son. Nearly one year later, Marshall himself met his untimely death.

With the information gathered from the gravesite and the interview with both the lightkeeper and John Piggott, Detective John Murray presented the facts to his supervisor in hopes of obtaining permission to open an official investigation. After a review of the situation, the high courts determined that an investigation should commence and the body taken to the coroner to be autopsied. Meanwhile, Detective Murray was granted permission to begin interviewing Port Rowan and Malahide locals, including Marshall Piggott's neighbors and relatives. Without haste, Murray made his way to the home of Marshall and John's mom, Lovina, where new information surfaced.

According to Lovina, a few days after Marshall's disappearance, a local man by the name of Havelock Smith arrived at her home. After a cordial greeting, Havelock produced a bank note made out to himself in the amount of $1,300. Havelock explained that he had lent Marshall the money a while back when Marshall was planning on traveling. He stated that he was now ready to collect on the IOU. Subsequently, he was hoping that Lovina could cover the check in the meantime. Lovina was suspicious of the story and asked Havelock where he originally obtained that amount of money. Havelock explained that he had borrowed it from Richard Chute, a prominent businessman in the township.

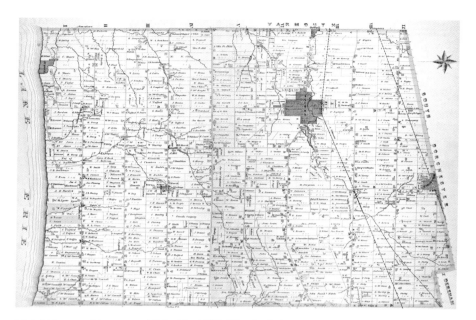

Malahide township map published in 1877. The shaded areas mark M. Piggott's property near the lake and H. Smith's property in close proximity. *From the* Illustrated Historical Atlas of Elgin County.

Following the money trail, Detective Murray learned that Havelock, twenty-nine years old, lived with his widowed mother on a farm near Marshall's farm and that the two men had struck up a neighborly friendship over the years. By most accounts, Havelock came from a "good" family. But near the time of Marshall's disappearance, Havelock displayed some unusual behavior.

Reportedly, in mid-November, Havelock rented a rowboat from a Mr. Pankurst at Port Bruce in order to collect his fishing nets tied along the shoreline. He made no mention of this expedition to his mother or brother, which was out of character, as the brothers usually fished together. Likewise, Pankurst found it odd that anyone would be retrieving fishing nets out of the lake this late in the year. Nonetheless, he rented the vessel to Havelock with directions to return it within a few days. It was not until December 3, nearly three weeks overdue, that the rowboat was found docked in the gully near Havelock's home.

Similarly, Murray determined that Havelock did not borrow money from Richard Chute, as he had explained to Lovina. Digging deeper into the finances, Murray learned that Marshall's farm had an estimated value

A postcard of Port Bruce, where H. Smith rented a boat. *Author's collection.*

of $1,300. He also discovered that many people coveted the valuable farm with its fertile land and easy access to the lake. Consequently, when Sarah, Marshall's wife, died from a mysterious illness, rumors circulated that someone may have wanted her out of the way in hopes of more easily manipulating Marshall.

As THE INSPECTOR CONTINUED to look into Havelock's activities near the time of Marshall's disappearance, he received word from the coroner that Marshall's cause of death was a blow to the head, as attested to by his cracked skull. Removing any doubt now, Detective Murray became even more determined to solve what was now a full-blown murder investigation, and all signs pointed in the direction of one suspicious individual. And it was not long before more incriminating evidence surfaced concerning that very person.

Murray learned that on November 17, Havelock was spotted on Marshall's farm around 9:30 a.m. At 11:00 a.m., both Havelock and Marshall were seen walking toward Havelock's property. That afternoon, two locals noticed Havelock walking through town wearing wet pants and carrying a shotgun. Havelock told the men that he was in pursuit of a gray fox near the gully on his property, but he did not explain why his pants were soaked.

When Marshall did not return, nearby neighbors assumed he went to visit his brother in Michigan, as he often talked about doing so.

On March 23, 1885, satisfied that he had enough evidence against Havelock Smith, Detective Murray had the suspect apprehended and placed in the St. Thomas Jail. While awaiting trial, Havelock's brother, a member of the city council, sought to hire prominent lawyers from the Ontario providence. Meanwhile, the prosecution prepared a case against Havelock for premeditated murder while continuing to secure witnesses and physical evidence.

Exactly one year and one week after the murder of Marshall Piggott on November 24, the trial of his suspected killer began at St. Thomas Courthouse with Chief Justice Armour presiding. The prosecution swore in over one hundred witnesses, including William Dickinson, Mr. Pankhurst, Detective Murray and dozens of residents. The prosecution theorized that Havelock Smith had lured Marshall Piggott to the gully, a secluded spot, to help him with the rented rowboat. When they reached the dock, authorities proposed that Smith hit Piggott over the head with a blunt object. He then rowed the body out through the gully, which fed into Lake Erie. Once in the lake, he weighed down his victim with heavy grates that he had swiped from

The St. Thomas Courthouse, where H. Smith was tried for murder. *Author's collection.*

Chute's Sugar Mill. When the defense argued that this was speculative, the prosecution produced its key piece of evidence.

While preparing for trial, authorities were sent to dredge the gully that flowed into the nearby lake waters after they learned that Walter Chute was missing a one-hundred-pound metal bar from his property. Years ago, a ship had wrecked off Port Bruce. As the wreckage washed on shore, Chute found several heavy metal grates, which he disassembled and carried back to his property, located north of Piggott's and east of Smith's. Not long after Marshall's disappearance, Chute realized that one of the bars was missing. When the team searched the lake, they retrieved not only the heavy bar but also a rope and Marshall's hat attached to a heavy rock.

The defense argued that the body found and buried on Long Point may or may not be that of Marshall Piggott. In their attempt to prove this, they were granted permission to exhume the body and hire a second coroner to examine it. The coroner suggested that there was no way of assessing whether the body was that of a White or a Black person or even if it was male or female. Nonetheless, the body did indeed show damage to the skull.

After closing remarks were made, with the prosecutors reminding the jury of strong motive and the defense insisting that there was doubt, the jury convened for deliberations. After several hours, a note was handed to the judge stating that no definite verdict could be reached. The trial ended in a hung jury.

Not satisfied with the results, the Canadian Crown ordered a retrial. In May, lawyers and witnesses found themselves once again in a long court hearing that lasted nearly four months. On September 22, 1886, once again, the jury delivered a note to the judge, and once again, they were deadlocked. After a second trial resulting in a hung jury, Havelock Smith was released.

In his retirement years, Detective John Murray wrote in his book of memoirs: "I read a lot of praise of the circumstantial case of the Crown against Havelock Smith. My mind is undimmed by a doubt on this case. Smith, the last I heard, still was around in that vicinity, and Marshall Piggott lies buried not far away."

If one "light" can be found in the sad tale of Marshall Piggott, it was that his body was returned to his family. Thanks to the efforts of one lightkeeper and one detective, Marshall Piggott was properly laid to rest.

5

LAKE ERIE HOAXES

SERPENTS, SINKINGS AND SIGNALS

Maybe it is the mystical appearance of the lake just before darkness falls, or maybe it is one of its rip-roaring productions during a summer storm. Perhaps it is the carefree feeling of a day spent on the lake. Possibly it is the long hours spent waiting for a fish to bite. Whatever it is, Lake Erie, as do many large bodies of water, tends to bring out the storyteller in many who gaze out over its surface. Dwight Boyer, a Great Lake historian, wrote: "Sailors, probably because theirs is a lonely trade, are a superstitious and pessimistic lot, forever pinpointing significant coincidences, dates or a sequence of happenings and building them into myths, legends and fables, most of which have acquired some degree of authenticity merely by their frequent retelling." Although many times these yarns are spun for the sake of entertainment or even a good laugh, they have potential to take on a more serious manner. Periodically, these tales circulate along the shores, building into a commonly held truth capable of causing fear and turmoil even for the most skeptical of receivers.

The Sandusky Monster

For centuries, the legend of a giant lake serpent plagued both sailors and land dwellers alike. Sightings of the creature were plentiful, as they are to this day. The mystical snake-like creature supposedly was rearing its dog-shaped head

MOONLIGHT ON LAKE ERIE, CLEVELAND, OHIO.

A full moon over Lake Erie. *Author's collection.*

long before the White man arrived. Native American tales include reports of a devil-spirited creature that lurked in the blue waters. Later, in 1793, the first written sighting occurred. By the early 1800s, as wooden schooners traversed the open waters, reports of a gruesome monster swimming about the lake made their way to the shore. In 1892, a run-in with a forty-foot beast by an entire steamer crew seemed to be the final piece of evidence needed for Lake Erie's monster to go from legend to fact. This sighting was reported in big-city newspapers, establishing it as real news in those days.

With the sightings publicized, the hunt for the legendary monster was on. Reports poured into newspaper offices, each story more frightening than the last. By the turn of the century, tales of encounters zipped across the lake from the American to the Canadian shores, with shouts from the islands in between. When there was a lull, newspapers were sure to fire up the rumor mill again. Thus, the BOLO (be on the lookout) alarm was sounded, and even the most cynical could not help but cautiously watch the waters just in case something was out there. Regardless of the plausibility of the tales, there was just something fascinating in each and every telling.

One tale that weaved its way through the western side of the lake and then into national newspapers occurred when two men had an apparent physical altercation with what was believed to be the Sandusky Sea Serpent. On the evening of July 21, 1931, Clifford Wilson and his friend Francis Bagenstose were leisurely night fishing in their rowboat in the eastern area of Sandusky Bay when they realized they were being quietly stalked by a water creature. They watched closely as the curious visitor made its way alongside the boat and then proceeded to raise its triangle-shaped head while exposing an elongated green, brown and white alligator-like hide.

Quickly, Clifford reached for his oar and gave the creature a heavy whack atop its head, immediately rendering the animal unconscious. Once the water stilled and then cleared, the men noted the incredible length of their opponent. Apparently, they had encountered a type of serpent, as its body stretched well past their boat. Realizing then that they had possibly incapacitated the notorious Sandusky Sea Serpent or a rare, nonnative species, they carefully tied a rope around its head and began rowing back to shore, their load a good few hundred pounds heavier than when they embarked.

The fishermen pulled their capture onto the bank, estimating that its body stretched nearly twenty feet across the pebbly beach. Fearing that the snake-monster would wake at any minute, the men quickly secured a large wooden shipping crate, which they hoisted, then shoved the animal inside and nailed it closed.

By the next morning, the word was out. Police Chief Leo J. Schifley of Sandusky, along with several newspaper reporters and an expert from the Cleveland Museum of Natural History, made their way to Thornburgh's garage, where the beast was being housed. Peering through the slats in the wooden crate, the party observed a gigantic snake-like species gazing steadily back at them. Based on its size, color and head shape, the museum curator, Dr. Madison, easily identified the creature as an Indian python, a nonvenomous species commonly found in subtropical areas of the world.

Later that afternoon, dozens of curious folks lined up in hopes of glimpsing the oddity still captive in its crate in the garage. Some speculated that the serpent was the culprit of the mysterious sightings in the western basin of the lake. Perhaps this was the face of the Sandusky Monster that had plagued the waters for years. Others wondered if the snake could be the missing python that had presumably escaped from a train car traveling from Barberton, Ohio, to Chicago a few months earlier. Purportedly, that snake grew tired of its travel accommodations, made a break for it and then slithered hundreds of miles to Lake Erie without detection. Others reasoned that perhaps it had escaped from one of the numerous circuses popular at that time of the year. No matter how or why the eighteen-foot, three-hundred-pound snake arrived in the bay, the excitement over its discovery was contagious.

Meanwhile, Chief Schifley learned that the fishermen were from Cincinnati, where they had been laid off from their jobs in a cement factory. They had been traveling throughout Ohio in attempts to gain any work available. While fishing for their dinner, they encountered the beast. Fortunately for these down-on-their-luck fellows, their catch of the day was proving to be more than just a meal ticket; the men were to exhibit their python at the popular Cedar Point Resort later that week.

For the chief, something about the story just did not sit right. For one, the beast's entrapment seemed quite effortless. Although Wilson and Bagenstose told the tale with a dramatic flair which emphasized their bravery, it seemed that the monstrous snake went down without a fight. To add to this theory, Dr. Madison suggested that the snake did not appear to have any injuries corresponding to a blow to its head. Second, for being penned in a proportionally tiny crate with dozens of humans about, the python remained docile and, at times, even friendly.

Finally, Dr. Madison pointed out that Indian pythons are commonly bought and traded among carnival exhibitioners, as they are the least threatening large-sized snake. With more questions than answers, Chief Schifley decided that further investigation was needed.

During introductions with famed fishermen, Clifford Wilson mentioned that he had a wife who was staying in Columbus with her uncle. Wilson also stated that the uncle, Al Nice, was the fire chief in Columbus. Following his instinct, Chief Schifley dispatched a call to Columbus, where he gleaned some telling information.

According to Al Nice, Clifford Wilson was his nephew from Alabama. Most interesting, Nice reported that Wilson had been traveling with a carnival that had recently stopped in Cleveland. As far as Nice knew, Wilson oversaw the house of mirrors and, of course, the reptile exhibit. Reportedly, Wilson had traveled with carnivals and circuses like his father before him. With this insight, the chief had a few more questions for the new local heroes.

The next morning, Chief Schifley returned to the garage, where several reporters were stationed. When Wilson and Bagenstose arrived, the chief wasted no time asking questions. Although the men stuck to their story concerning the python's entrapment, they remained silent regarding their connection to the carnival. Likewise, when asked about their job loss with the Cincinnati cement company, the pair provided vague answers.

With the promise of returning, the police chief made his way back to the station, where he continued his quest. After a few conversations with his Cleveland connections, he learned that the city had recently hosted the Cleveland Shriners Convention, which included concessions and performances from a traveling carnival. One crowd favorite was a lovely eighteen-foot Indian python, like the one captured in Sandusky Bay a few days after the convention ended.

By evening, the word was out concerning the inaccuracies in the story. Crowds gathered outside the Hotel Rieger, where the two showmen were lodging. However, when crowds arrived, they learned that Clifford Wilson was missing, as was the snake. According to Bagenstose, Clifford went to Cleveland to arrange for advertisement in the city newspapers. How and why he transported the snake with him could not be explained. Soon after Schifley grilled Bagenstose, it was discovered that Bagenstose had left town as well.

Over the next twenty years, accounts of a giant python on display cropped up across the country. In the summer of 1931, the Rubin and Cherry Show in North Carolina showcased a twenty-foot python named Goliath. According to Goliath's keeper, a Dr. Welliever, the snake was the famed serpent caught in Sandusky Bay after it had escaped from Welliever's show in Cleveland. By winter of that year, the creature had made its way to St. Petersburg, Florida, where its owner, Clifford Wilson, captivated crowds by telling of the time the snake broke free in Ohio. He recalled that two cement salesmen had captured it. Wilson quietly went to Sandusky to retrieve the snake by feeding it cats. In 1936, the Royal American Show exhibiting in Edmonton, Canada, shared some exciting news with local reporters. The Sandusky Serpent was now a mother of fifty-six snakelets, a rare occurrence for a snake in captivity. Crowds were encouraged to attend the show that evening and visit the snake exhibit, where the Curator of Sea Lore, A. Bagenstose, would provide more information about the new mother and her offspring. Ten years later, Clifford Wilson, an attendee of the national Showmen's League Convention held in Chicago that year, told the tale of his prized possession, a python named Tickey. He recalled a time during a Cleveland show when Tickey became quite moody and placed Wilson in a triple scissor hold for forty minutes before making a break for Lake Erie. The snake, apparently tired of show business, spent thirteen days in the lake, eventually making her way to Sandusky Bay, where she was promptly retrieved. In 1954, in one of the last purported displays of the Sandusky Monster, a twenty-foot python named Phyllis made the news in Fort Worth, Texas. Here the famous Sandusky snake was displayed with Pete, another giant python that had run away from the zoo and made his own headlines a few weeks prior.

reptile was com-
mproved the oc-
skin, or scaling,
leeping.
it necessary to
i or it would get

Left: Clifford Wilson and his assistant place a muzzle over a python after it attacked Wilson during a show. *From* American Weekly, *1936.*

Below: An illustration of the python attack. *From* American Weekly, *1936.*

Meanwhile, back in Sandusky, locals continued to tell the story of the day the Sandusky Monster was captured. Today, local newspapers occasionally run an article on the event, particularly when a new sighting of the lake monster is reported. For the small lakefront community, the yarn became the best local fisherman's tale of all times.

Message in a Bottle

In the early days of Great Lake shipping, ship-to-shore communication was nonexistent. Prior to the Wireless Ship Act of 1910, if a ship was floundering, there was a good chance the captain, crew and passengers were on their own unless they happened to be spotted by a passing vessel or a lifesaving station from shore. Anyone in such a situation was aware of their potential fate and sought to somehow get a message to land. Whether a plea for help or final words to loved ones, these messages often came via a note placed inside a container. Because of the serious nature of such communications, the finder of a message in a bottle usually handed the item over to local authorities. Consequently, when a medicine bottle washed ashore hinting at the truth about the most mysterious Lake Erie shipwreck of all time, the item was immediately handed over to the proper officials.

On May 7, 1928, a beachcomber noticed a tiny glass medicine bottle half-submerged in the sand on a Port Stanley, Ontario beach. Inside the bottle, a note was tightly folded. On inspection, the finder could faintly make out the words. Scrawled on the backside of a magazine cover was a message declaring that the missing car ferry *Marquette & Bessemer No. 2* could be found exactly fifteen miles southwest of Port Stanley. The finder recognized the name of the ship. Even though the ship had gone missing nineteen years earlier, the tragedy and mystery were still fresh in everyone's mind, especially those living in Port Stanley, where the ship had been set to dock on its fateful voyage.

On December 8, 1909, the crew of the massive *Marquette & Bessemer No. 2* had set out on another routine run. The weather had been unseasonably mild, allowing for a longer shipping season, and this particular morning was no exception. Still, like many ships traversing the water this late in the season, the threat of a notorious nor'easter storm was always just over the horizon. Nonetheless, the forty-degree temperature for that day promised an easy voyage. Thankfully, as the crew of thirty-six loaded approximately thirty train cars at the port in Conneaut, the lake provided a smooth backdrop.

By 10:30 a.m., all systems were go, and the *M&B2* begin its normally five-hour jaunt toward Port Stanley. If all went well, the crew would make port by 4:00 p.m., unload and be home by 11:00 p.m. Yet a few hours into the expedition, the crew noticed the fast-moving clouds being ushered in by a high-powered front. Within a couple of hours, the temperature had dropped by thirty degrees. The waves began a rage of protest again the now hurricane-like winds.

What happened during this storm on the final voyage of the *Marquette & Bessemer 2* is a confusing web of eyewitness and onshore accounts. Some experts believe that the captain tried to make it to port in Ontario. When that proved impossible, he most likely ordered the ship to be turned around and headed back for Conneaut. That would explain why people on both sides of the lake reported hearing the distress horn at one point or another. People in Port Stanley claimed to have heard the cry around 1:00 a.m., yet people in Conneaut insisted they heard the whistle around the same time. Other ships out on the lake around the same time reported seeing the *M&B2* at various locations on the lake. For weeks following the incident, reports continued to bounce from the United States to Canada like a ping-pong ball. With the numerous accounts and after days of searching, rescuers were unable to locate the massive ship.

On December 11, a small steamer sailed through a debris field off Long Point. Later, it was determined that the wreckage pieces were that of the *M&B2*. Since the debris had floated in rough waters for five days, the wreckage offered no indication as to the location of the hull.

On December 12, about fifteen miles off Erie, the *Marquette & Bessemer 2* lifeboat number 4 was found drifting, carrying in it nine bodies. Newspapers reported that four of the corpses were frozen in sitting positions and another four were huddled on the floor over a body, as if trying to keep it warm. Also, a set of clothes was found frozen to the bench of the lifeboat, suggesting that another passenger had made it on to the boat only to bail or fall off sometime in the chaos. Heartbreakingly, the fate of the crew was certain. Mysteriously, though, the colossal ship, as long as a football field, fifty-five feet high and loaded down with thirty-plus train cars, still remained missing.

Subsequently, when a message noting the ship's resting place was found on the shore at Port Stanley nearly two decades later, it was considered a serious matter. At least, at first it was. It did not take long for authorities to realize that it was a hoax. First, the note was written on the back of what appeared to be a modern magazine. The handwriting, although faint, seemed not to have any signs of sunlight or water damage. Second, the bottle itself was

6

WILLIAM TOWNSEND

CATCH ME IF YOU CAN ON THE GREAT LAKES

Get your facts first, and then you can distort them as much as you please.
—*Mark Twain*

Unlike murder, the transportation industry had been a part of his life since his beginnings. Growing up in Port Dalhousie, Ontario, William Townsend regularly watched as the huge ships moved in and out of the Welland Canal, a system built to connect Lake Erie and Lake Ontario. As the water vessels arrived, the sound of train whistles was not too far behind as they chugged into the port to either load or unload their own cargo to be moved about the canal system. Often, William had a perfect observation deck, as his father, Robert, a skilled carpenter, was hired to help build the huge wooden docks at the port. Even when the construction was finished and his father retreated to a livelihood based on farming, William was often found along the canal or near the shoreline of the lakes, observing as ships, trains and buggies hustled about the ports. No one ever predicted that the quiet, wide-eyed little boy would one day rely on his knowledge of the Great Lakes transportation network to escape his violent crimes and leave two countries sailing in a sea of mystery and controversy for centuries to come.

The first child born to Robert and Mary Ann in Fort Porter, New York, in 1828, William was accustomed to both hard work and life along the water. Robert, a descendant of Sir Roger Townsend, who helped settled Plymouth,

Map of the Niagara Peninsula, where the Townsend Gang carried out its crimes. *Courtesy of Brock University, Map, Data, and GIS Collection.*

was a well-respected carpenter and shipwright. Mary Ann modeled great perseverance and strength, as she had lost both her first husband and brother during the War of 1812. Eventually, the family moved across the border to the Niagara Peninsula, which was once called Upper Canada. There, Robert secured work on the first Welland Canal. A few years later, he purchased farmland in Canfield, near the center of the peninsula, and the family settled into a life of farming.

As William grew into his teens, it was apparent that life inland never seemed the right fit for him. After all, he had spent the first decade of his life on the banks of one of two Great Lakes, the Niagara River and the canal. Therefore, at the age of thirteen and with the support of his family, he applied for work on a Royal Navy ship, most likely one that he had admired from afar throughout his childhood. In 1844, he was officially employed to work in the galley of the famed SS *Mohawk*. For two years, instead of standing along the docks watching the ships, he proudly stood on the decks of one of the grand vessels. Although he was stationed in the kitchen for long hours, he often found time to wander throughout the ship, learning the ins and outs of maritime life. As the crew moved about the waterways, William visited new ports and became a master of Great Lake geography, skills that would prove invaluable to him within a few years. Unfortunately, his happiness was shattered just two years later, in 1846, when he received word that his father was deathly ill.

Returning home, William tended to the family farm while his father suffered in bed for the next few months. In his time in the hot fields, it is likely that William's dislike for farming was reaffirmed, as he made no attempt to claim his right as the man of the house on his father's death later that year. In fact, it seemed that something had hardened in William following his father's funeral, as attested to by later reports from his relatives. Soon after, William abruptly left the farm to return to the one place he felt at peace.

Back on the water and now aboard the SS *Montreal*, fifteen-year-old William entered training as "second-class boy" with the Royal Navy. Second-class boys were males between the ages of fifteen and seventeen of both good physical and moral condition who agreed to serve the Royal Navy, usually for twelve years, following their apprenticeship on a training vessel. Moving quickly through his training, William became a skilled and knowledgeable sailor. But it seemed that the confines of military life were too much for him. The newly trained seaman deserted both the Royal Navy and the SS *Montreal* after only two years.

After leaving his station, William returned to work on the SS *Mohawk*, possibly in search of the happiness he once felt on that ship. By all accounts, he was a good worker and even received the affectionate name of "Little Davy Crockett." However, only two months in, while docked in Cleveland, William uncharacteristically refused to help paint the bottom of the ship and disappeared into the city crowds.

During the year of 1848, William resurfaced on his family farm. Only occasionally helping with chores, William was most often found completing odd jobs at the Welland Canal. Sometimes, he was spotted on the barges helping to unload. Other times, he assisted with the towing in and out of large ships. At one point, he worked as a cooper, building barrels and other such storage containers used in transportation. For a short while, he worked as a stagecoach driver, transporting passengers from Hamilton to Cayuga. As he moved from job to job, it seemed that William never could quite find his life's calling. He continued his restless search into his early adulthood years.

It was during this quest for both identity and a livelihood, from 1850 to 1854, that William became involved in two hobbies that would greatly impact his life. First, from the time he was a child, William had an extraordinary gift in that he could accurately mimic almost anyone he encountered. This included mannerisms, dialects and intonations. As the tiny towns grew into large industrial hubs all around the Niagara Peninsula, William used his acting skills and musical talents to entertain crowds and earn a few extra pennies. Second, just as the opportunity for show business increased with the population surge, so, too, did the chance for street crimes. As a result, gangs lurked about the alleyways and country highways looking for unsuspecting victims. While William aimlessly roamed about the bustling ports, it was not long before he became affiliated with a local group involved in pickpocketing and petty theft.

Made up of young men who were known for their rowdy drinking, the restless pack included seven official members: Lettice, King, Blowes, Bryson, Patterson, Weaver and Townsend. Initially, the gang, operating along the lakeshores and small villages, started out as a run-of-mill group of bullies and thieves. Gradually, as time wore on, the violent nature of the crimes escalated, building to a fateful home burglary that would change the course of the lives of all involved.

On the night of October 18, 1854, several members of the group were spotted at their favorite watering hole in Cayugo. Later, many witnesses would testify that Townsend was not much of a drinker but that he did enjoy carrying on with his colleagues as they imbibed. Whether over their shots of whiskey or after they departed into the night, the gang members made the decision to head west, toward the small rural village of Nelles Corners.

Around 10:00 p.m. that evening, with the chilly air gently blowing in from nearby Lake Erie, the men silently crept down the road leading to the village. Aided by the moonlight, they soon could make out the target among the few buildings making up the small town. Within minutes, they were at their destination: the general store and attached house of John Hamilton Nelles, a prominent businessman known to keep money on the premises. Approaching the house, the gang momentarily paused as they noticed the dim light still shining in the front room of the living area. Not deterred by the potential of someone still stirring about the home, three of the bandits continued to the door while two covered the outside. With three heavy knuckled knocks, the men impatiently waited for the occupants inside to respond.

Startled, John Hamilton Nelles, the last of his family still awake, jumped from his chair where he had been reading. As he tentatively creaked the door open, he comprehended at once that this was not a friendly social call or family matter, based on the haphazardly disguised faces of the three men standing on his doorstep. He quickly slammed the door, only to have it flung open again by the agitated invaders. Waving shotguns, they demanded that John hand over any money in the house. Refusing to do so, John sealed his

Nelles Corner in the late 1800s. Nelles' General Store and home is shown on the right. *Courtesy of Haldimand County Museum & Archives.*

fate, as the man with a pasted-on crocked mustache swiftly lifted his gun and unloaded three shots point blank into him.

Hearing the deafening commotion, other members of the household began to stir. John's wife and mother of their infant daughter and his sister-in-law sprang into the front room. Seeing John on the floor with his shirt saturated in blood, Mrs. Nelles dropped to her knees in an attempt to aid her semiconscious husband while the sister stood paralyzed in fear. Ignoring the women, the three intruders began to ransack the house. When they noticed John's fourteen-year-old brother, Augustus, peering from the kitchen doorway, they commanded that he tell them where any valuables were hidden. Not garnering an answer from the frightened lad, the men continued in their quest. They were only able to uncover John's expensive pocket watch hanging from a nail. With the frantic search for treasures coming to an end, the mustached man glanced at the barely breathing John and yelled, "You scoundrel, you slammed the door in my face!" Three hours later, John died from his wounds.

The next morning, when Constable Campbell in Cayuga learned of the night's events, he immediately formed a team and headed toward the farm country. There he was quickly informed that two additional robberies had taken place on the road leading back toward his town. During these two robberies, five bandits matching the descriptions of John Nelle's killers had accosted farmers completing chores in the predawn hours. Much like highwaymen, the gang hid in the nearby woods and then jumped their victims as they passed by to their fields.

Heading back toward town, the constable learned the criminals had been spotted at the Canfield Train Station and possibly boarded the early morning train to Buffalo. At this point, Constable Robert Flanders from a nearby town had gathered up his own team and volunteered to follow the trail eastward. When they reached Buffalo around 4:00 p.m. that day, they contacted the city police. Fanning out, both the Canadian and American forces scoured the city, but to no avail. All signs indicated that the gang had circled back and exited the way they had come.

Returning to Ontario empty handed, Flanders was not to be discouraged, and he expertly picked up the trail again. Within a couple of days, the lawmen learned that a man had sold a pocket watch at the port in St. Catharines. After identifying the watch and obtaining a description of the man trading it, they realized that they were closing in on William Townsend, who had just boarded a ship by the name of *Westchester* that was bound for Oswego, an American port on Lake Ontario.

Once again, Flanders found himself in a mad dash. But this time, instead of racing a train, he and his team were up against a ship that had a more direct route to the port. Luckily, Flanders arrived just in time to meet the ship as it docked in Oswego, thanks to the rough seas that day. Climbing aboard even as it was being tied up, Flanders and his men upturned every crate and barrel on the vessel, but they had no luck finding a hiding criminal. It was only while questioning the captain that the officers learned that a man matching Townsend's description had embarked at St. Catharines, but he had disembarked at Port Dalhousie and boarded a different vessel bound for Kingston, an Ontario port. It appeared that William Townsend had skillfully slipped through their fingers by using his maritime education.

Fortunately for the authorities, while Townsend was busy hopping back and forth across the border, three of his colleagues had remained in familiar territory. King and Blowes were found in Hamilton, with Blowes shacking up in a "house of ill fame." Soon after, Bryson was located and apprehended near Toronto. He was the only one with the cleverness to leave the county. With three of the bandits captured, authorities were now confident that the last two robbers would soon be apprehended, as authorities had garnered additional clues from men in custody.

Here it is important to note that in the 1850s, the Canadian government, the Crown, was aware of increasing occurrences of crimes on the Niagara

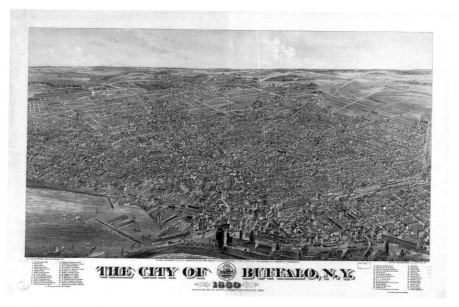

Buffalo Harbor in 1880. *Courtesy of the New York State Library Digital Collections.*

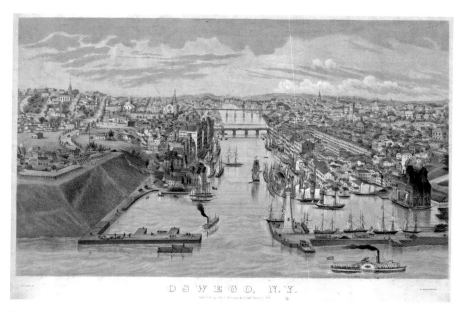

Illustration of Oswego Harbor in 1860, where Townsend fled the police. *Courtesy of the Library of Congress.*

Peninsula. Because of the upswing in criminal activities, higher-level agents were often sent to investigate, as the Crown meant to demonstrate swift justice to end the current crime wave. The Nelles murder case was no exception, and so the solicitor general of Canada (similar to the American director of the FBI) was sent to take over the Townsend situation. Not only was Townsend wanted for murder, but he was also considered an armed and dangerous highwayman.

Most likely, William and Lettice, the last of the gang, were traveling together, according to the new information at hand. On October 2, a report came in that a wheat farmer had been robbed on a secluded road on his return home to Port Robinson. All signs pointed to the dynamic duo, based on the nature and method of the crime. Likewise, it was learned that Townsend had relatives in that area, and it was likely that he was hiding there. Rumor had it that he may be disguised as his sister Elizabeth, whom he resembled.

After taking a statement from the wheat farmer, Jacob Gainer, local police learned that the men were probably headed straight to Port Robinson in hopes of boarding a ship or train. During the afternoon, Port Robinson constables Charles Richards and James McCoppen found that two men matching the fugitives' descriptions were spotted at the Jordan House and were currently enjoying a dinner courtesy of the farmer they had robbed.

Without haste, Richards and McCoppen entered the inn and immediately located a man they believed was Townsend seated at the bar. When approached, the bar patron exchanged pleasantries with the officers and explained that he had never heard of a person by the name of William Townsend. Not falling for the nonsense, Richards attempted to apprehend Townsend. With customers looking on, Townsend demanded that Richards back off or else. Paying no mind to the threats, Richards clamped down on Townsend's arm as Townsend struggled. In a blur of motion, Townsend broke free and swiftly whipped out a pistol. Without hesitation, he shot the unarmed Constable Richards and made a break for the door while witnesses sat frozen in fear.

In the days following, a large reward was offered for information on Townsend and Lettice. It was believed that the men were now working separately. Perhaps because Lettice was not as skilled as Townsend in disguise and evasion, he was tracked to an isolated island in the Niagara River known as Squaw Island. Here he attempted to hide atop an abandoned barn but was shot and killed.

In the weeks following, it is believed that William Townsend hopped a train on the Great Western Railroad in Hamilton bound for Windsor.

Authorities at Woodstock, a small village on the railway line, believed that Townsend was hiding inside a train car. When they arrived, they raided the car and found a man that resembled the fugitive and pulled him from the train to the platform. Already surprised by the appearance and politeness of the groggy stowaway, they were further taken aback when he looked directly at the policemen surrounding him and explained that they must have him mistaken for that rogue, Townsend. Furthermore, the pleasant fellow told the police that this was not the first time there had been such a mix-up, as he had been identified as Townsend in the previous town on the line. Sadly, as much as he would like to help the hardworking lawmen, the man explained that he could not be Townsend, as he was merely passing through town from Rochester, New York.

While the constables discussed their plan of action, the train began its steady chug from the station. The man in question seemed unconcerned and even joked about missing his train. Seemingly, the detainee was willing to forgive the officers for delaying him in his travels, at least for a few minutes. Later, one constable explained:

> He was so well dressed, and had such a smile on his face, that I did not arrest him. I went to take counsel with the other constables, and when I went into the car again he was gone.... We saw him again afterward, on the platform, and concluded we would detain him. He said it was very hard, for he wanted to go west. We said it would only be for a short time, for people were coming on the next train who could identify him. He then stood still while the train was moving away, but, as it had attained a good rate of speed, he darted away like a deer and jumped on the last platform of the last car, leaving us behind.

Once in Windsor, he most likely boarded one of dozens of ships and set sail across the Great Lakes region. Knowing the transportation system inside and out, Townsend was able to evade capture for the next couple of years. Meanwhile, his colleagues paid the price for their involvement in the crimes.

In April 1855, Knowles, King, Blowes and Bryson were tried by the Ontario Courts. Blowes and King were sentenced to death and later hanged. Bryson was sentenced to life in prison in exchange for his testimony on the murder and various criminal activities associated with the Townsend Gang.

Over the next few months, tips continued to trickle in concerning the whereabouts of William Townsend. One of the most promising was that he was traveling with an American circus, Stone and Van Amburgs, as a sideshow actor. In this case, Constable Flanders traveled hundreds of miles to the States, only to have the man in question disappear.

With his ability to travel throughout the Great Lakes system in two separate countries as well as completely disguise himself, it seemed that the infamous murderer and highwayman had vanished into the misty lake air. Yet, two years later, just as authorities were about to give up, a mysterious individual surfaced who would be held accountable for the violent acts committed on the Niagara Peninsula.

On a warm April afternoon in 1857, an irritated train conductor for the Bee Line Railroad, a line connecting Columbus and Cleveland, entered the New London Hotel in Cleveland. Accompanying the conductor was a man appearing somewhat nervous as the pair approached the business owner, John Lies, who was drying glasses at the bar. The conductor explained that the man had hopped his train somewhere along the way and now owed $3.50 fare, which he was unable to produce. Instead, the unwelcomed passenger had offered his revolver as collateral until he could pay his way.

As John Lies, who had just moved from Ontario to the States, looked closely at the rail hopper, the glass that he had been drying slipped from his grip and smashed to the floor as realization set in. Freighthopping was the least of the crimes committed by the confused-looking stranger standing in his bar. For Lies was certain that he was looking at none other than the deadly highwayman, William Townsend, for whose capture there was a handsome $5,000 reward. Without delay, the bartender bolted outside to flag down the beat cop who frequently passed by the bar.

First to arrive to the New London Hotel was Office Gallagher. After hearing the accusations from both the barkeep and the conductor, he turned to the man in question. The gentleman explained in a heavy accent that he had never heard of this William Townsend. His name was Robert John McHenry and was an immigrant from Scotland passing through on his way back East. As more officers arrived on the scene, Mr. McHenry elaborated that he had only been to Canada once, when he arrived in North America at Quebec. From there, he made his way straight to the United States and began work on ships that sailed all over the world.

As they gathered around the man, the group was divided as to whether to buy his story or not. With hesitation, the Cleveland officers decided to arrest this McHenry fellow and let the higher courts figure it out. If he was indeed the elusive Townsend, known to escape the law at every turn, they were not taking any chances. With this, they hauled the now agitated fellow off to the city jail to be dealt with accordingly.

While awaiting his fate within the dank walls of his cell, McHenry was visited by local lawmen and curious onlookers alike. At one point, the police requested the aid of a clairvoyant, who was certain the man's auras displayed the hues of an evil murderer. Eventually, Constable Flanders from Ontario arrived in hopes of gathering Canada's most wanted man, but after a grueling interview with the inmate, he was unable to determine the man's identity.

Newspaper reporters in both countries clamored for information to print on the Townsend/McHenry saga as their divided readers hungrily read each article for tell-tale clues to the puzzle. Ultimately, the most intriguing information came from a letter written by the prisoner himself. During an interview with a reporter from Haldimand County in Ontario, McHenry passed his visitor several pages of writing and asked that he print it in his newspaper. Not only did the lengthy letter express the prisoner's growing agitation, but it also showcased that the man was well educated, based on his writing and vocabulary skills.

On June 10, 1857, after spending nearly two months in prison, the man writing under the name Robert J. McHenry expressed his own opinion in the matter in his open letter to the editor.

In Jail, Cleveland, Ohio, Monday, June 1, 1857—

Mr Editor—Ever since I was arrested on the 11th day of April, 1857, charged with being William Townsend, the murderer of one Nellis, in Canada, I have been subjected to endless insults and annoyances.

For weeks after I was arrested, crowds of people of all conditions rushed into the jail to gratify their morbid appetites for the wonderful, gazing at me with feelings similar to those entertained by little boys when looking through the bars at the untamed "Gyasticutus." A hundred and fifty policemen from all parts of the Union with their pockets filled with descriptions of "murderers", "pickpockets", "burglars", and desperadoes of every description have intruded themselves into my cell, to discover if possible that I was a great criminal escaped from somewhere. But none of them have recognised me or seen me before anywhere, they say.

A number of witnesses who knew Townsend came here to see me, and unhesitatingly expressed their opinion, after a full opportunity to view me, that I was not the man Townsend, and after being put in training, bamboozled and bedevilled by the virtuous policeman of this city, they came into Court and swore that I was the man, and that, too, without having seen me, since they had said positively I was not what they swore I was.

The papers of this city have very unjustly prejudiced my case, forestalled and created public sentiments, misrepresented the evidence, and some of them announced, without knowing one word of me or of my history, that I was surely Townsend the Murderer, and that further, if I was not Townsend, I was surely some other great criminal.

The letter continued with several more examples of the injustices, mistreatment and misunderstanding over his predicament. Although seemingly heartfelt, and of course well expressed, the letter served to divide the public further, but it did nothing to shorten or eradicate his time in custody. Instead, a few days later, Mr. McHenry was extradited back to Canada to be tried for his crimes.

On September 27, 1857, the trial for the murder of John Nelles began. Before prosecutors could even begin to produce evidence for or against the accused, the matter of identity first had to be settled. For days, dozens of witnesses were called to the stand in hopes of proving that the man seated in the courtroom was indeed William Townsend. Former employers and Townsend family members insisted that the man was not William, while former friends, including gang member Bryson, and townsfolk were certain that he was one and the same. Members of the Nelles family who witnessed the murder could not be sure, as the men were disguised the night the crime took place. Lawmen, too, were divided as they questioned the man who eloquently denied that he was not the notorious highwayman.

Finally, the judge determined that there had been adequate testimony and that the jurors had to decide if the accused man, regardless of his real name, was guilty of the murder. Naturally, the jurors were as confused and as divided as the public and, after seven hours, reported that they were unable to reach a definite decision.

The prisoner was then sent to await trial in Welland County for the murder of Constable Charles Richards. While awaiting trial in his cell at St. Catharines, he again penned a letter

Artist's replica of newspaper illustration of Townsend/McHenry during court hearings. *By Avery Milhoan.*

to the media, suggesting that his situation was a source of entertainment and form of monetary gain for society. "As I always was of an enquiring turn of mind, my experimenting propensity had a beautiful opportunity to prove what amount of corruption there was in the country; what a corrupt and degraded press would bring forth, what the love of a few paltry dollars would weigh in the scale of human integrity and justice, for I could see as plain as day their objects to prostitute the truth, and sell me, if they could, for the reward."

In addition to his declarations of extortion, the prisoner provided specific details of his whereabouts before the Townsend ordeal ever began. Specifically, he iterated that he had very little knowledge of Canadian geography, as the country was a mere stopover when he arrived in Quebec in 1837 as a young boy. From there, he went on to the States and began work on ships. In fact, the closest he had been to the location of the crimes occurred in 1852, when a storm on Lake Erie forced the crew to take cover in the mouth of the Grand River on the Ontario boarder. Therefore, his lack of geographical knowledge should be telling of his innocence.

Although his letter did nothing in terms of convincing the Crown of his innocence, it did accomplish something. First, as the public read McHenry's words, more doubt began to seep in throughout the community. Not only was the author of the letter persuasive, but he was also clearly sophisticated. Second, the specifics of his journey during the previous decades provided the defense with concrete evidence, as they were able to acquire witnesses on behalf of McHenry.

On March 26, 1858, after serving nearly a full year in one jail or another, the prisoner was escorted back to stand trial. Although the Crown, the solicitor general and the courts sought to avoid a repeat of the first trial, the same issue emerged: Was the person charged William Townsend, Robert McHenry or neither?

Again, dozens of witnesses were brought to the stand. This time, though, the defense brought stronger proof that the man was Robert McHenry and had no connection to the murder. Accusations flew back and forth, creating an entanglement of testimony for and against the accused. On the tenth day, with the trial finally ending, the jury was sent away to deliberate. After twelve long hours, they came to a verdict. They agreed that the man was Robert McHenry and, therefore, could not have committed the homicide.

Later that day, the acquitted walked out of the courtroom a free man, but one forever in question. As he faded into the Great Lakes landscape, his story continued to circulate into the next century.

In 1918, a justice of the Supreme Court in Toronto reexamined the case. In his findings, published in the *Journal of Criminal Law and Criminolgy*, he wrote the following.

> *The most extraordinary criminal case in many respects in Upper Canada was that of "a person charged with crimes committed by William Townsend." In his research, he reports that the Townsend Family received a letter from William after the trials that he was working on a ship that traversed Lake Erie. Later he wrote he was called to notably fight in the Civil War although no evidence of this has ever manifested. In 1921, William Wallace Sewart, considered an expert in Canadian history, proposed the idea that the man on trial was neither Robert McHenry nor William Townsend. Instead, it was very likely that he was a deserter from the British Army in Canada.*

Articles of national interest on both sides of the lakes periodically appear to this day, most hinting that the skilled mimicker, expert sailor and evil murderer William Townsend conned his way to freedom by using his knowledge of the Great Lakes systems.

7

LYING IN WAIT

THE TRIPLE MURDER OF KELLEYS ISLAND

It is the mental poise of the wild beast in quest of prey, and necessarily implies
malice, premediation, deliberation, and willful intent.
—*State vs. Tyler, 1904*

J ust after midnight on September 19, 1911, the man crept into the potato patch on the north side of the island. This was not the first time he had done so, but it would unknowingly be his last. His mission, as ordered by the unoffical leader of the house, was to swipe a few of the end-of-season vegetables to feed himself and the four other men living in the boardinghouse. When he bent over to yank a plump oval from the ground, he never saw the dark figure pounce from its hiding place, nor did he have time to react when the knife was plunged into his back. An hour later, when the man's brother came in search for him, he, too, was not given the opportunity to defend himself before a bullet blasted into his chest.

Although many states have adopted the term *premediated* or *aggravated* to define the preplanning of a crime, a more fitting phrase was used in earlier courtrooms that better connotated the calculating nature of the actions leading up to the deed. The phrase *lying in wait* as found in the research of Mitchell Caldwell was first used in American courts in 1794 and then adopted into a Pennsylvania state law in 1904 declaring that a person found lying in wait would not be eligible for pardon. In 1990, Indiana Supreme Court justice Roger Debruler vividly detailed both the mental and physcial deviousness involved in such a crime.

There is considerable time expended in planning, stealth and anticipation of the appearance of the victim while poised and ready to commit an act of killing. Then, when the preparatory steps of the plan have been taken and the victim arrives and is presented with a diminished capacity to employ defenses, the final choice in the reality of the moment is made to act and kill. This...circumstance serves to identify the mind undeterred by contemplation of an ultimate act of violence against a human being and, of equal importance, the mind capable of choosing to commit that act upon the appearance of the victim.

When Dominic Selvaggio and Rocco Klawetch were found guilty of "a homicide that was committed purposely with delibirate and premediated malice" in 1912, the jury clearly understood the sinister cunningness involved before, during and even after the murders. And when the judge handed down the maximun punishment of death by the electric chair for both men, he as well comprehended the level of evil exercised when a human predator lies in wait to kill his prey.

According to Rocco Klawetch, the plotting of two of the three murders commenced in August 1911, one month prior to the crime. Klawetch, one of five italian immigrants employed by **Kelleys Island Lime and Transport Company**, had helped his roomates, brothers Jan and Paetri Beril, count their money, which they kept hidden in the house. Klawetch reported that the brothers had trouble understanding American denominations, but he had learned quickly. He recalled that the brothers together had a sum of nearly $600 that they were saving in order to return to their homeland, Calabria, Italy. Soon after, Klawetch told Dominic Selvaggio and Antonio Discarie, his other two housemates, of the hidden money. That very night, Selvaggio and Klawetch excitedly began to mastermind the robbery and necessary murder of the Beril brothers.

Once the plan was established, or "the preparory steps had been taken," the next item on the checklist was to lure the brothers away from the clustered rental homes, where someone would likely overhear the scheduled ordeal. Fortunately, the island abounded in secluded, dark areas, but the trick was to entice the targets to go to one of these places. This was an easy fix; Selvaggio simply barked an order at Jan Beril to go swipe some grub from the nearby potato patch. Although Selvaggio was reportedely tiny in stature, all five men in the boardinghouse looked to, or perhaps feared, him as the leader of their small domain. Without question, Jan slipped on his shoes and headed out into the midnight air.

Kelleys Island Lime and Transport Company. *From the Charles E. Frohman Collection, Rutherford B. Hayes Presidential Library & Museums.*

From a short distance, Selvaggio stalked his unsuspecting victim as both predator and prey made their way down the wooded path leading to the gardens. On arrival, Jan set to the task of locating a few plunp potatoes, while Selvaggio crouched in the thicket between the woods and the patch. Just as Jan kneeled on the ground, unknowingly positioning himself in the most vulnerable stance, Selvaggio lunged from his hiding spot. In one swift movement, he plunged a knife into his target. Most likely, Jan never had a chance to look into the eyes of his friend-turned-killer as Selvaggio continued to stab him over and over again.

When the deed was done, Selvaggio calmly returned down the path, his only fear that someone may have heard the scuffle just moments earlier. Approaching his boardinghouse, he picked up the pace until he was in what seemed a panic run. Barging through the door, he exclaimed that Jan had been shot by the owner of the potato patch and was in desperate need of help. As Paetri Beril cried out in horror at the news concerning his brother, the caring and ever-attentive Selveggio attempted to calm down the openly sobbing man and explain that all of the housemates would go to the garden to assist in the matter. Swiftly, Selvaggio, Klawetch, Discarie and Paetri Beril hurtled down the path in attempts to save their suffering friend and brother.

On their arrival at the garden, the three in cahoots allowed for Paetri to charge ahead while they hung back a few feet. At this point, Selvaggio whipped a gun from his pocket and took aim at the distracted man. When Beril stopped to make sense of the noise, it was apparent that Selveggio had missed. Before anyone could make another move, Klawetch grabbed the gun from Selveggio and fired it straight at Beril's chest. This time, the surpised man collapsed on the ground not far from his brother's bloodied body.

Seeing that both brothers were dead, the remaining three housemates hightailed it back to the house, where they discussed the next steps in the diabolical plan. It was in these discussions that Selvaggio suspected that there was a troubling glitch in the operation that he had not accounted for in his meticulous planning. As the hours wore on, both Selvaggio and Klawetch noticed that Antonio Discarie began to show distress over the the situation and his involvement in it. This was quite surprising to them, as Discarie had more experience and notority in crime than the other two put together.

Before arriving on Kelleys Island to work in the quarries, Discarie had served two years of hard time in Elmira Prison in New York for his dealings with the Black Hand Society. The organization, composed of Italian gangsters, operated several extortion rackets by threatening well-to-do families with bodily harm, kidnapping, property damage and sometimes death if demands were not met. The threating letters, usually marked with a black hand, were sent via the U.S Post Office. Technically speaking, the murders at Kelleys Islands seemed simple compared to the Black Hand operations, so it seemed unnatural that the supposed gangster would be distraught now.

Perhaps it was fear of returning to prison, or maybe, just maybe, Discarie felt some remorse for the brutal slayings. Whatever was causing the ex-con to act off-kilter was not the concern. The real issue was that his fidgety, anxious behavior could blow the cover, and Selvaggio intended to put a stop to it before that happened. Pocketing a nearby razor blade, he kept a close eye on Discarie, whom he now considered the weakest link.

In his third and final murder of the night, Selvaggio stuck to his cowardly formula: wait until the victim was in the most incapacitated state and then strike. This had worked well during the first two, and the murderer was certain that this time would be no different as he stood over the sleeping Discarie. Like a lightning strike, Selvaggio thrust a razor blade into Discarie's throat and sliced horizontally from ear to ear. Pulling back, he could see the man's eyes shining in the darkness. Unlike the brothers, though, Discarie, even with blood pouring from his jugular, tried to strike back. He leapt from his bed and, swinging into the darkness, attempted to fight off his attacker but was met with several blows. Moving into the hallway, the fight continued near the top of the stairs. Somewhere in the madness, Discarie lost his balance and tumbled to the bottom, never regaining consciousness.

With their main objectives complete, Selvaggio and Klawetch began the final phase: the cover-up. In the initial outline, the pair had planned a quick disposal of two bodies. The potato patch was located just a few yards from the lake, a fact not lost on the ever-calculating Selvaggio. Dragging the bodies to the shore, they tied each to large boulders, easily found on the rocky north side of the island. With the brothers heavily weighed down, they tossed them into the lake from the high cliffs. The splashes were muffled by the choppy waters breaking against the walls.

At this point, their work for the night should have been completed, but there was still the issue of an additional dead body lying at the foot of the steps in the boardinghouse. Running out of darkness, they decided that the fastest disposal method would be to discard the body off the beach near their camp. Although this was not an ideal choice, as it did not offer the remoteness of the first dumping area, it would have to do. Following protocol, they tied Discarie with ropes, attached him to a large rock and dragged him into the lake.

Returning home, the pair quickly dressed for their workday at the quarry. The idea was to lay low for a few days as if nothing had happened. When the time was right, they would make their way off the island and return to their home country—the motivation behind the robbery in the first place. Believing the plan was foolproof, the murderers were surprised a week later when events began to turn on them.

For all the careful planning, it seemed that the duo had underestimated the power of the lake current and its ability to carry even large items to the surface. Near the end of his confession, Klawetch stated that "we did not think they would ever come up, and so we stayed at Kelleys Island working right along until the first one washed ashore." With this turn of events—or tides, in this case—the men made a break for it.

Frustratingly, Klawetch's desire to "make peace with God" came over a year after the fact. Because his detailed confession came after he received the death penalty, it seemed Klawetch only wished to save himself from eternal damnation, as he had withheld most of the information during his trial. It was only after a full-blown investigation, lengthy trials and retrials and an appointment with the chair that he revealed the heinous details of the crimes. Prior to this, it was left up to local lawmen and the courts to piece together what had occurred on an otherwise peaceful island.

When several quarry workers pulled in the naked body that was spotted floating just offshore, it was apparent that it was a product of murder. Not only did the corpse have ropes tied to the hands and feet, but it also was covered in contusions. Most telling, of course, was the wide slit across the man's throat. The body was taken to the Kelleys Island undertaker, William Berger, who called in the Erie County sheriff and coroner when he determined a crime had occurred.

As news spread around the small island, locals speculated that the murder most likely took place on one of the ships passing through. After all, it appeared that no one was missing on initial questioning. Violence of this nature was almost unheard of, and locals preferred it to remain that way. Yet, when Sheriff Herman Reuter arrived on the scene, his hunches told him otherwise, based on the trail of blood he found on the beach. A day later, when the body was identified as Antonio Discarie, a similar blood trail was found leading out the front door of his home, confirming that a murder had indeed taken place on the island.

It was soon determined that Discarie's four roommates, also Italians, were mysteriously missing. The initial thought was that the five men may have had a fight over money, with the four ganging up on Discarrie and then headed off the island. Sheriff Reuter quickly picked up a trail at the Marblehead-Danbury Train Station when he learned that at least two Italian men had booked passage soon after news of the murder was out. The train master also made mention that they had sent their luggage, which consisted of a large trunk, ahead to Cleveland. On September 27, the sheriff, along with a foreman from Kelleys Island Lime and Transport Company needed for identification purposes, headed east in hopes of finding the suspects.

On arriving in Cleveland, they feared they had met a dead end, as the men or anyone fitting their descriptions had not been seen. What they did learn was that the trunk had been sent forward to Pittsburgh, Pennsylvania. Following this lead, the sheriff and foreman proceeded to Pittsburgh, where local authorities were eager to aid in the search.

Because the suspects were believed to be Italian, local authorities were able to provide two resources that proved invaluable. First, they offered insight into the demographic layout of the city. Several sections of the city had become meccas of Italian immigration over the past half century, including Oakland, East Liberty, the Lower Hill District and Bloomfield. These areas were known to host single men from southern Italy who were seeking work and often traveled back and forth between the United States and their home country. Second, the Pittsburgh Police Department called in

Detective Angelou, known for his work in the Italian population. With his connections in the community and with tips from the train station, Detective Angelou led Sheriff Reuter to a westside neighborhood.

While authorities worked to locate the suspects in Pittsburgh, two more bodies were found by a fisherman while he was casting near the northside shoreline on September 28. Like the first body, the second and third both showed signs of a violent death. Within hours, they were identified as the Beril brothers, two of the missing housemates. The island was now looking at a triple-murder scenario, the first in its history.

On September 30 at 1:00 a.m., Sandusky and Pittsburgh police raided a small boardinghouse in the East Liberty neighborhood. At first, the two surprised men attempted to make a dash out the back door but realized it was heavily guarded. Resignedly, they gave up the fight. They were handcuffed and taken to the Pittsburgh jail. While awaiting booking, their only plea was to be extradited back to Italy. A few days later, on October 5, they were moved, but not across the ocean. Instead, they were taken to the Erie County Jail to await their trials.

Unlike today, the trial was scheduled a little over a month later, on November 22. It was determined that each man would be tried separately, beginning with Rocco Klawetch. Using a court-appointed interpreter, Klawetch answered the questions thrown at him by Prosecuting Attorney Henry Hart. He maintained his innocence throughout the trial. When the jury read the verdict twenty-seven hours after the closing statements, they found Klawetch guilty with a recommendation for life in prison as opposed to the death penalty, as one juror was not convinced that a death penalty was warranted. Against his lawyer's advice, Klawetch sought a new trial based on several technicalities, including the lack of eyewitnesses and language translation issues.

During his second trial in June 1912, Klawetch surprisingly pled guilty and admitted to killing Paetri Beril. His ploy to appear as an honest man who simply made a mistake did not go over well with the new jury. This time, when the verdict was read, all jurors recommended the death penalty. The judge ordered Klawetch to be put to death by electric chair at the Ohio State Reformatory.

Dominic Selvaggio's case was similarly complicated but did not result in more than one trial. Basically, he had no information concerning the murders. Understandably, he was quite confused as to the bloody mess and clothes found at the boardinghouse. As for leaving the island on the day that Discarie's body was found, he easily explained that coincidence as well; the

No. 42 Domminick Sellvagio
Of Erie County. Electrocuted November
22, 1912, for the Murder of
3 Italians.

No. 41 Rocco Klawetch
Of Erie County. Electrocuted November
15, 1912, for the Murder of
3 Italians.

Left: A portrait of Dominick Sellvaggio taken after his trial. *Courtesy of the Ohio History Connection, Ohio Department of Rehabilitation and Corrections Collection.*

Right: A portrait of Rocco Klawetch taken after his trial. *Courtesy of the Ohio History Connection, Ohio Department of Rehabilitation and Corrections Collection.*

island climate was bad for his rheumatism, and he was planning to return to Italy with a stopover in the Italian village in Pittsburgh. Unfortunately for Selvaggio, the jurors were not confused over the evidence, nor did they care about his arthritis. On December 22, 1911, he was found guilty of murder in the first degree and sentenced to the electric chair. Later, he would be granted two reprieves as he continued to fight for his innocence.

Fittingly, the two men who had laid in wait for their victims had plenty of time to wait for their appointment with the chair. Klawetch was executed first, just after midnight on November 14, 1912. Prior to his death, he sought counsel with his spiritual advisor, sent a letter to his family in Italy and sent a message to his dear friend Selvaggio. A week later, on November 22, Dominic Selvaggio, clutching a crucifix, was led to the death chamber. His final wish was that he be buried in Italy, but that was not to be. Just after midnight, Selvaggio was strapped to a chair, where a meticulously planned amount of 1,750 volts was sent through his body.

8

JOSEPH KERWIN

THE LAKE ERIE PIRATE

J oseph Kerwin never considered himself a pirate. In fact, when he was convicted of piracy on the high seas, in this case Lake Erie, in 1904, he was not only surprised but also somewhat relieved. Sure, the crime carried a hefty penalty, but he would much rather go down labeled an infamous buccaneer than carry a moniker that hinted at the real evil within him, an undiagnosed and untreated malevolence that had lived in him since his childhood.

Perhaps the "bad" seeds were planted early on, as he experienced the ways of the world from the rough side of Toledo. In 1881, when he was only one year old, his father died of illness, leaving his mother, Margaret, an Irish immigrant, to provide for four young children. As their mother scraped out a living by first working as a maid and then operating a boardinghouse, the children observed life from their window overlooking the Tenderloin District of Toledo, what was once considered the red-light district of the small city.

In his book *Hidden History of Toledo*, author Lou Hebert describes this part of Toledo.

> *The Tenderloin District was a segregated area of businesses and homes near downtown, where life was lived on the wild side. A place where one could buy most anything to satisfy the cravings of flesh. If you wanted it, it was probably for sale. It was its own city in a way, which operated independently of the laws that governed morals and vice in the city, and it was a magnet for those who sought to live their lives on the tattered hems of society, if only for a few hours a week.*

It was in this area of the city that Joseph fell in step with those around him and was eventually charged with his first crime.

It came as no surprise that a young lad of the streets would be apprehended for delinquent behavior, as this was a common occurrence. What should have been alarming, however, was the nature of that behavior. At the age of fourteen, Joseph was charged with attempting to strangle a teenaged girl. The solution was to send the boy to a reform school, where he could work off his transgressions. Surely, the hard physical labor and strict education would work out whatever wickedness was within the child, hopefully reforming him into a law-abiding citizen by the time of his release, set for two years away.

After serving his time, Joseph made his way to Chicago. Once again, he returned to the streets to make a living by any means possible. Returning to his comfort zone on the rougher side of a city, he found himself drawn to the only lifestyle he had ever known. As he reverted to his old habits, the darkness began to overtake him. At the age of sixteen, it became too much for the teenager, and he attempted to strangle yet another young girl in 1895.

At the turn of the century, criminal psychology was still in its infancy, and little, if any, work had been done concerning youth offenders. The idea was to reset the mind of teenagers who could not behave themselves. Evidently, this had not worked for Joseph Kerwin the last time, so perhaps a longer sentence would serve him well. This time, he was sentenced to four years in the Illinois State Reformatory in Pontiac. A school, according to the research findings by Sarah Millender, was built as "a place for the thorough reformation and elevation of the erring young people of our State."

For a few years after his release in 1899, it appeared that perhaps Joseph had been reformed and elevated. He married and assumed gainful employment as an oiler on the lake steamers. Likewise, he began to study for a mechanical engineer certificate after the birth of his daughter. Returning to homestead in Toledo, perhaps to be close to his mother and siblings, it seemed as though Joseph was on the right track.

Unfortunately, in 1902, accounts of an evilness lurking in the city began to infiltrate the Toledo Police Station. Around Christmas of that year, a young woman reported that she had been attacked by a man who attempted to strangle her. On January 26, 1903, another woman awoke to find a man standing above her. The next time she woke, she was choking up blood in her empty bedroom. Later that month, Anne Snyder, reportedly of the Tenderloin District's "underworld," was found strangled to death. As police looked for the perpetrator, clues trickled in, eventually naming the guilty party as "Joe the Choker," but the trail turned cold over the next few weeks.

Illinois State Reformatory. *Author's collection.*

In this same period, the city of Cleveland was on the lookout for its own "choker." In this case, the suspect was known as "Jack the Strangler," perhaps in reference to a more infamous Jack, of Whitehall, London. On February 13, police responded to a call at 119 Lake Street, where they found the lifeless body of Maggie Snedegar, who had been asphyxiated to death in the brothel house. Based on a ransacked trunk found in her room as well as her reported missing wristwatch, it seemed that this was a case of a robbery gone bad. Nonetheless, the Cleveland Police still had a violent murder on their hands, and they were looking for someone with a penchant for choking women.

While police followed up on tips, Maggie was laid to rest in the nearby Woodland Cemetery with only her aging father and the caretaker in attendance. According to friends and the madam of the Lake Street house, Maggie had left her home in Huntington, West Virginia, two years prior to her arrival in Cleveland, where she wished to find work. Maggie had claimed that she and her stepmother did not get along, but she did love and miss her father and younger sisters, as attested to by photographs of the family and letters found in her room. Sadly, the most recent letter from her father was found under the door the same morning her body was discovered.

On February 23, ten days after Maggie's murder, a call from Lake Street came in from a Helen Morris, who stated that she had been attacked by a man who had tried to strangle her. As the police scoured her home for clues, another report interrupted the search. The caller stated that she was the mother of Belle Anderson, and both women had just been assaulted. Shockingly, they had their attacker sequestered in a back room at 151 Lake Street.

Immediately, the police made their way to the location just a couple of blocks away and apprehended the trapped man, who gave his name as Joe Kerwin. After a search of his person, they found a woman's watch, which later was found to belong to Maggie Snedegar. Likewise, Helen identified the man as the one who had attacked her just hours before his capture. Based on this evidence and the nature of the crimes against Helen Morris, Belle Anderson and her mother, the police believed that they had Maggie's killer in their custody.

Joseph's arrest made front-page news in both local and national papers. As police in Toledo read these accounts, they wondered if the incarcerated man might be their infamous "Joe the Choker." Consequently, Joseph's photograph was shown to the young women who had been attacked in their city. Without hesitation, both victims identified the man as the one who had accosted them just weeks prior to the arrest in Cleveland. Toledo police also suspected Joseph as Anne Snyder's murderer, but they did not have enough evidence to arrest him.

In May 1904, the trial of the "Cleveland Strangler" began. The prosecution's burden of proof for the murder of Maggie Snedegar was two-pronged. They first pointed out that Kerwin had been identified by Helen and Belle and two women in Toledo as their attacker, suggesting a pattern of violence. They then called the person who had supposedly gifted the watch to Maggie. This person positively identified it as the one he had given the deceased.

On the other hand, the defense argued that Joseph was of good character and a hardworking family man. This was evidenced by his young and openly weeping wife, with newborn in tow, at every trial session. They also showed that the watch found on his person was not expensive or unique and could belong to anyone. The final, and strongest, argument came from a doctor. The doctor determined that Maggie had suffered from Bright's disease, which, in his opinion, could easily have been the cause of her death, especially compounded with her unhealthy lifestyle.

On the afternoon of June 5, Joseph was led back to his cell to await the verdict. Finally, around 9:30 p.m., the jailor unlocked the cell door and informed the prisoner that it was time to return to the court for the reading. Joseph was found not guilty of the murder of Maggie Snedegar. The next morning, the acquitted Joseph told the *Cleveland Plain Dealer*: "It was the worst nine hours I've ever put it. When the jailor called me…I thought he was joshing me. Well, I started to put on my shoes, and my feet and hands shook so I could hardly get them on. And then when the verdict was read, I was simply stunned for a moment. I would have been less at a loss for something to say if they had convicted me.…I guess that I will get my wife and settle down to work, just as soon as I can get rested up a little."

With the ordeal behind him, Joseph and his small family moved to Detroit. During the 1904 summer season, Joseph secured work with the Detroit and Cleveland Navigation Company as an oiler on its recently built passenger steamships. Plying between Detroit and Buffalo with stops at ports in between, the D&C's sister ships, the SS *Western States* and SS *Eastern States*, offered sleeping accommodations, dining and entertainment aboard the luxury liners. These overnight trips, consistent schedules and frequent tasks kept Joseph steadily employed and seemingly on the straight and narrow for a short time. But, just as there is a repeated pattern for steamers traversing across the lake, it seems there is also a predictable one for serial offenders as well.

The SS *Western States. Courtesy of the Library of Congress.*

LAKE ERIE MURDER & MAYHEM

On the morning of September 13, 1904, the SS *Western States* was due to dock at its Detroit slip. As harbor workers awaited the steamer, they noted that it was unusually late in its return. Soon, family and friends who came to fetch passengers lined the docks. Shielding their eyes from the sun and watching to the east, they were relieved to see the nose of the ship peeking over the waves. As the ship neared the dock, however, it slowed its engine to a halt, leaving the vessel and all of its passengers idling in the harbor. Soon, word was sent from Captain McDonnell that a police officer was needed to assist prior to disembarking.

The first to arrive on the scene was Detective Frank Wilkinson of Detroit and Special Agent Newton of the D&C Line. The investigators learned that at approximately 1:00 a.m. on her return home from Buffalo, a passenger by the name Adelia C.B. Sweeting was startled awake in the darkness of her berth. As she struggled to make sense of her surroundings, she realized that a man was standing over her. Before she could react, the man placed a cloth over her nose and mouth and attempted to strangle her with his free hand. According to Adelia, she lost consciousness within seconds of the attack. When she came to, she sprang from her bed, flung open her cabin door and ran to the open deck. There, while choking and gasping for air, the terrified woman caught the attention of a crewman on duty. Although Adelia could barely speak, the man realized from the purplish-blue marks on the woman's neck and her panicked state that something horrible had occurred. Unsure of how to help, the sailor led the woman to the captain's quarters, where she shakingly explained what had taken place.

Accounts vary regarding the captain's initial reaction to the situation. Some reports state that the captain was of the belief that Adelia was mistaken and attempted to brush her off. If true, this may have been an attempt to protect his ship's good reputation, a common desire for any captain. Eventually, after the second mate reported that the cabin had been ransacked and showed signs of a struggle, the captain supported Adelia's claims of a robbery and a possible attempted murder. Others say that Captain McDonnell took sympathy on the victim from the start. Either way, by daybreak, he was fully convinced that a violent criminal was aboard his ship, and the plan was to keep him from leaving before help arrived.

As Detective Wilkinson questioned Adelia, he learned that three diamond rings had been taken from her fingers during the attack. Likewise, forty dollars were missing from her purse. Her description of her attacker was quite vague, as it had been dark, but she was certain that the intruder was tall. On further investigation, it was learned that there were no signs of forced entry into the locked cabin, which led the detectives to believe that the crime may have been committed by someone who had access to cabin keys. With this, he asked to meet with all employees on the steamer.

While interviewing the deckhands, sailors and mechanics, the detective learned of the crew's whereabouts and job duties during the night's voyage. Reportedly, all were performing routine tasks. He noted that the crew was quite forthcoming and wished to be as helpful as possible in the investigation. But this general assessment of a smooth-sailing, tight ship changed when he re-questioned the mechanics onboard.

During the first round of questions, the detective had observed that one of the oilers, Joe Kerwin, was extremely nervous. During the second set of questions, the man was visibly shaken. Sure, it was normal to be anxious during a police investigation, but this Kerwin character had Detective Wilkinson's senses on alert. Digging deeper, he learned that the oiler had just recently transferred from the SS *Eastern States*, sister ship of the SS *Western States*, which was not uncommon, but still pointed to a nuance in the routine operations of the SS *Western States*. And when he learned that Kerwin had been seen returning from the upper decks shortly after Adelia's attack, his inner alarm bells sounded.

Meanwhile, Special Agent Newton was informed that Joe Kerwin had been caught stealing from the galley pantry by using a pass key, which he should not have had in his possession. The staff changed the locks soon after the event. Also, supervisors reported that they had ordered the oiler from the upper decks on several occasions after he was found lurking about the passenger commons.

Not having enough to hold their suspect, the investigators allowed Kerwin to disembark. While they continued to investigate, another matter arose concerning the jurisdiction of the crime. Because the shipping lanes in Lake Erie run near the border between Canada and America, determining the nation in which the crime took place was of upmost importance. Once navigation records were reviewed, it became clear that the SS *Western States* would have been in American waters at the time of the attack. Therefore, the person responsible, if caught, would be tried in the United States.

When the case was turned over to federal investigators, they determined that the crime fell under the maritime law of "crime on the high seas"— more specifically, piracy—and was punishable under the Federal Criminal Code of 1790.

If any citizen shall commit any piracy or robbery aforesaid, or any act of hostility against the United States, or any citizen thereof, upon the high sea, under colour of any commission from any foreign prince, or state, or on pretence of authority from any person, such offender shall, notwithstanding the pretence of any such authority, be deemed, adjudged and taken to be a pirate, felon and robber, and on being thereof convicted shall suffer death.

While the feds sorted out the jurisdiction matters, Detective Wilkinson continued his own quest into his suspicions concerning Joseph Kerwin. On September 14, he made a house call to the Kerwins' ramshackle tenement at 144 Antione Street in Detroit, where he found Mrs. Kerwin, severely sick, home alone with a young child. When questioned about her husband's recent activities, she explained that the day before, he had returned from work with forty dollars that he claimed to have won while gambling with the crew on board. Later that day, after hearing about the robbery on the ship, she pleaded with Joe to return the money, but he became furious and stormed out of the apartment.

With this information, the detective canvased the neighborhood, focusing on local pawn and jewelry shops. He hit paydirt within a couple hours of his tour when he learned that Kerwin had been in John Hellerich's fine jewelry store on nearby Michigan Avenue attempting to sell three diamond rings matching the description of the stolen ones. Circling back to the Kerwin residence, he was delighted to find his suspect at home.

Although Joseph did not receive his guest with a warm welcome, he did not seem surprised or fight the appearance of the lawman at his door. Getting right down to business, Detective Wilkinson presented Joseph with the evidence stacking up, including his suspicious behavior on the ship and the stolen money and jewels. For a short time, Joseph presented a weak attempt to deny his guilt. But as the policeman pressed on, and with his wife's encouragement, Joseph finally confessed to the robbery and attack on Adelia Sweeting. Defeatedly, he handed over the rings and the reaming thirty dollars in cash that he had stashed in his pockets.

While local authorities processed their prisoner for intake, federal prosecutor William D. Gordon took a closer look at the suspect and his dark past. Not only had the twenty-six-year-old man been accused of a murder-robbery the previous year, but he had also been in and out of the system for similar crimes for over a decade. Adding to the already thick file of Joseph Kerwin, a new report came in from a woman when she read of the recent crime on the SS *Western States*.

The victim, Mrs. W.C. Mason of Elmira, New York, explained that just a week prior, she had sailed on the SS *Eastern States*. Sometime in the middle of the night, she heard a knock at her cabin door. When she opened it, an unknown man attempted to push his way into her room. As she pushed back, the two landed in the hallway, where she was able to reach a panic button. The assailant fled down the corridor, but not before Mrs. Mason got a good look at the man. She was certain that the intruder was the same man described in the newspapers.

Prior to the start of Joseph's trial, Adelia Sweeting sued the Detroit and Buffalo Navigation Company for $25,000 for neglect and poor treatment aboard the SS *Western States*. Adelia stated that the cabin boy assigned to her hallway would have had to have heard her cries for help. She also attested that Captain McDonnell had originally dismissed her account as a hallucination. During the proceeding, D&B Company superintendent Schantz stated that he had learned prior to the trial, that some of his staff had "not shown every courtesy." They were immediately terminated from his payroll. In the end, the court ordered that the company pay $12,000 to Adelia Sweeting.

On December 3, a more thrilling trial began. Joseph was led to the federal courtroom of Judge Henry Swan of Michigan's Eastern District Court, where he pled guilty to the crime of robbery on the high sea. Judge Swan, surprised at the admission, as it carried the maximum punishment of a hanging under U.S. laws, reiterated the technicalities of the jurisdiction. Had Joseph committed the crime on Michigan land, it would have carried the charge of grand larceny with a penalty of a few years' imprisonment. On the other hand, had Joseph made the choice to carry out his act in Buffalo's waters, he would most assuredly be put to death, as the state carried a mandated death penalty for piracy. Siding somewhere in the middle of the various penalties, Judge Swan sentenced Joseph to life imprisonment.

As the infamous pirate began his new life inside the Detroit House of Corrections, he lived up to his reputation of rebellious criminal. According to the *Lansing State Journal*, "he was far from a model prisoner" during his seven-year stint at Detroit. In 1912, he was transferred to Leavenworth Federal Penitentiary in Kansas. Not only did his physical environment change for the better, but supposedly his moral convictions did as well, as he explained to the parole board in 1913. "I am literally born again, mentally and morally as well as physically. My mind has changed, my ideas of right and wrong have changed with my body. By a system of reading and thinking I have taken on a new moral nature. You are now punishing the body and mind I have today for what the body and mind I had eight years ago did."

Although Kerwin did not receive his parole in 1913, it appeared that during the decade of his sentence he sought to make right his wrongs. While in prison, Joesph began correspondence courses toward an electrical and mechanical degree. He perfected his love of music by becoming an accomplished trombone player and performed in prison skits and plays. His love for the arts eventually led to the esteemed postion as editor-in-chief of the *New Era*, a small publication inside Leavensworth Penitentary. In addition, he became well known for his poetry and was named the poet laurete among the prisoners.

> *CHOOSE WISELY by Joe Kerwin*
> *TRUTH'S Chalice, heaven-sent and aureoled,*
> *Is poised. 'Tis yours to have of God's reward*
> *You opportunity; Time may not hold*
> *The Cup for aye; Tommorow might unfold*
> *A sombre sorrow sharpened as a sword.*
> *The Chalice holds the guerdons of the Lord—*
> *His promises engraved in angel-gold.*
> *THUS Heaven meets you at the morn of life,*
> *To give ev'ry blessing of the day.*
> *Choose wisley when earth's turbulence of strife*
> *Assails you as you walk along the way.*
> *The Chalice holds the true Divinity—*
> *The Wine of Good—The Sacred Trinity.*

At his 1926 parole hearing, several factors were in Kerwin's favor. Not only had piracy penalties become outdated, but Joseph Kerwin also had established a near-perfect reputation, which was attested to by fellow inmates, prison personal and social service professionals. By all accounts, the once violent priate had truly been rehabilitated. After serving twenty-two years for his crime, Joesph Kerwin was released on parole.

Unfortunately, factors on the outside were not in his favor. First, the likelihood of returning to a life of crime was and is high for previous offenders. The first recidivism study in 1923, by social scientist Lloyd Warner, found that "the greater the number of previous crimes committed by a delinquent, the greater likelihood of recidivism." Second, although Joseph proclaimed and believed he had changed mentally and morally, he had never been treated for his mental health issues. Leaving the predictable routine and stability within the prison system, where he had flourished, would have been

94

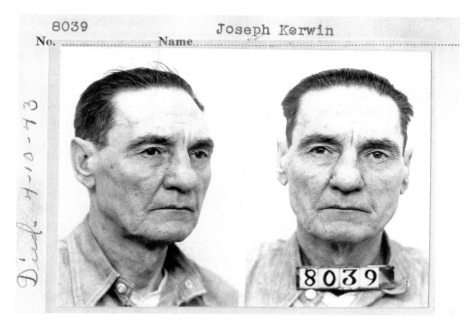

Booking photo of Joseph Kerwin in his later years. *Courtesy of the National Archives, Department of Justice, Bureau of Prisons. U.S. Penitentiary, Leavenworth.*

an extreme adjustment. Consequently, a few years later, perhaps "when earth's turbulence" assailed him, Joseph Kerwin did not "choose wisely" and was sent back to Leavenworth Penitentiary on a burglary conviction. He lived out his days as a model prisoner until his death in 1943.

In his early years of imprisonment, Joesph told the *Denver Post* that "I do not wish to be placed in criminal history as a monster in disguise, a cutthroat and muderer." Instead, the man once known as "Joe the Choker" and the "Cleveland Strangler" went down as the only convicted pirate of the Great Lakes in modern history.

9
THE TOLEDO SPEEDBOAT DISASTER OF 1930

For two days, the Coast Guard and special Prohibition agents patrolled the area known as Ward's Canal near Bono, Ohio. The canal and the swampy marshes adjacent to it was a well-known hotbed for rumrunners. However, unlike most stakeouts during the summer of 1930, agents were not looking for the typical smugglers. Instead, they were looking for eight prominent Toledo businessmen who had mysteriously disappeared without a trace.

Two days earlier, on the morning of June 14, 1930, the Toledo Yacht Club was abuzz with early season activity as the promise of a beautiful summer day stretched out across the lake. Although the lake was still a cool sixty-two degrees, the sun warmed the air and created a glittering effect as far as the eye could see. As the eight men climbed aboard the twenty-six-foot Dart speedboat, they could not wait to slice out across the majestic blue waters.

Aboard the boat that day were Charles Nauts of the IRS Toledo Division; his son Herbert Nauts; Franklin Jones, president of Acme Coal; Henry Hainbuch, a city sanitation engineer; Arthur Kruse of Burman-Kruse Mortuary; Frank Miller, city heating engineer; John Meyers, the owner of the speedboat; and John Liptak, the pilot. For these men who spent so much time and energy in the confines of the city, a boating excursion offered an ideal escape.

The plan for the excursion was to head northeast to Pelee Island, where the gentlemen would attend an Elks picnic. Not only was the area perfect for fishing, but it also was in Prohibition-free Canadian waters, which added

7 TOLEDO YACHT CLUB, BAY VIEW PARK, TOLEDO, OHIO

5A-H1866

The Toledo Yacht Club, where the missing men departed bound for Pelee Island. *Author's collection.*

another appealing benefit. Loaded down with picnic essentials, including six slabs of bacon and top-of-the-line fishing gear, the crew set out at approximately 10:00 a.m.

Not long after takeoff, the crew was spotted jetting into open waters near Maumee Bay. According to passengers on the steamer *Greyhound*, also bound for the Elks picnic, the speedboat was traveling at a high rate of speed. Two passengers on board the *Greyhound*, both friends of John Meyers, were surprised to see the boat zipping by at nearly thirty miles an hour. To them, it seemed out of custom for the experienced boat pilot, yet they realized that a little showing off on a speedboat was not unheard of among their fellow boaters. What they did not realize was that this would be the last time anyone would see the eight men alive and well.

EIGHT HOURS LATER, AT 7:30 p.m. that evening, a Dart speedboat was found floating adrift near West Sister Island. Immediately, the Coast Guard realized that something was amiss. For one, the boat was left in the forward gear with the throttle wide open. Second, the glass windshield was shattered completely. It would later be discovered that the tow line had been cut with a knife and the rudder was bent. Also, after further investigation, it was determined that of the six slabs of bacon, only three remained. Most alarming, there was no sign of anyone, dead or alive, near the boat or island.

The next morning, it was determined that the deserted boat was indeed the craft that had carried the eight Toledo men. With still no word from the men, search crews were quickly formed to begin a massive hunt for any sign of them. By Sunday afternoon, several recreational boats, Coast Guard vessels, ships and small planes scoured the western basin of the lake in hopes of finding anything to indicate the men's whereabouts. Islands, including West Sister, Put-in-Bay and Pelee Island, were searched thoroughly as well, in the event that the men had made it to land. But nothing materialized during these initial searches.

By Monday morning, search crews could be spotted as far as the eye could see. Local people came to help in the search. Additionally, President Herbert Hoover had ordered the U.S. Treasury Department to lend aid in the search, allowing for more agencies to assist. With all eyes toward the water, finally, one clue emerged.

On Monday afternoon, a local search party spotted something floating about four miles off of West Sister Island. As they made their way to the object, they realized it was a flotation device. After sweeping it into the boat, they determined that a shirt was attached that bore the initial "CHN," for Charles H. Nauts. Yet, even with this latest development pointing toward a possible boating accident, authorities still remained puzzled, as no bodies had been recovered. As the sun sank into the dark blue water, hope of finding the men began to drop as well.

By Tuesday morning, with optimism waning, a new theory began to circulate that gave call to a great alarm. Apparently, Walter Nauts, another son of Charles, received a message from a reliable source in Cleveland that the eight men had been kidnapped by a party of rumrunners-turned-pirates. The message indicated that the "underground telegraph" system had been active for two days with information on the kidnapping. Apparently, four hours before the abandoned speedboat was found, a group of alcohol smugglers from Bono had been looking for it in hopes of hijacking the party. Reportedly, the men were being held in captivity somewhere in the vicinity of the abduction. Luckily, authorities had a pretty good idea where to look.

Ward's Canal, located in Bono, Ohio, which is thirteen miles east of Toledo, was a well-known hideout for local rumrunners. The canal and the adjacent Bay Shore swampland, now Metzger's Marsh, provided everything a person in the business could need. The steep walls of the canal as well as the heavy vegetation of the swamp offered coverage as well as quick and easy lake access, especially for those traversing between the Ohio and Canadian border, just a few miles out from the mouth of the canal.

Immediately, search vessels descended on the canal, including local sheriffs, Coast Guard patrols, police and Walter Nauts. The search was fueled by the belief that the missing men were known to have valuables in their possession, including men's diamond jewelry and large amounts of cash. It would not be out of the question to assume that their disappearance was a result of a robbery gone wrong.

A few hours into the search of the swamp and the canal, however, the searchers received word of a vital development in the case. In the late afternoon of June 18, the body of John Liptak, the speedboat pilot, was recovered a few miles from West Sister Island. Crews were instructed to abort the search in the swamps and summoned to assist with a search for more bodies near the island.

While the retrieval of John Liptak's body offered some clues to the mystery, it also presented more questions. First, Liptak's wristwatch had its hands stuck at 10:50, indicating that he had entered the water shortly after the speedboat left the bay. Likewise, the wristwatch most likely stopped working due to impact as opposed to water damage. This indicated that perhaps the boat hit something in the water and threw the men overboard. But if Liptak or the others on board had been swiftly tossed overboard, how did Liptak manage to have on his life preserver?

Over the next week, other bodies were retrieved, with Charles Naut being the last. Notably, John Meyers, known to be a prolific swimmer, was found closest to West Sister Island, suggesting that he had tried to swim for the shoreline. Most of the men were found in only their underwear, as they had removed their clothes in order to swim without restraint.

Yet even with the retrieval of the bodies pointing to a boating accident, rumors persisted and questions remained.

For one, there was the speedboat left fully intact, minus a broken window and bent rudder. If the boat had hit something at a high rate of speed, many experts believed that it would have capsized. The fact that it was found in the upright position was enough for many to question the theory of an accident.

Second, the entire western basin of the lake was infamous for anti-Prohibition criminal activities. From the rumrunners hiding out at the canal and swamp near Bono to the notorious Purple Gang lurking in the area, chances of crossing paths with someone in the industry were at an all-time high. A group of wealthy men carrying cash and valuables could easily fall prey to anyone looking to make some fast cash in the open water.

Last, the event seemed eerily familiar to some. Nearly twenty years earlier, a group of eight Toledo businessmen and politicians set out on a fishing trip on September 2, 1911. Leaving the Toledo Harbor, a mile and a half from the Toledo Yacht Club, their small vessel, the *Nemo*, was struck and cut in half by the freighter *Philp Minch*. Seven of the men drowned, pulled under the water as the vessel sank. The *Nemo* disaster was deemed an accident at the trial and by public accounts, but the characteristics between it and the 1930 events were strikingly similar.

Although the Toledo speedboat tragedy is officially considered a boating accident, many to this day argue that there is a mystery to be solved.

10

MARY APPLEBEE

ALL THE MOURNING DAYS BELOW

Sometimes, the worst crime that a person can commit is to go against his or her own instincts.

Throughout history, mariners relied on superstitious, omens and dreams as a means of guidance across treacherous waterways. When signs appeared to them, they would often charter or recharter a course based on their beliefs in hidden meanings. Either no one explained this to Mary Applebee, or perhaps it was her Christian upbringing against such notions, because all signs suggested that she should have never boarded the ship.

For weeks, Mary had horrific nightmares of a shipwreck. In her dreams, she could not find her way off a ship that she was certain was sinking. For what seemed like hours, she clawed and scraped her way through floating, broken pieces of the crumbling vessel. And every night, right before she was startled awake, the ship would lurch violently, signaling its defeat. Several years later, in 1833, the dream, along with several other premonitions, would resurface in Mary's mind when she found herself clinging to life within the bowels of a sinking ship, praying that she would wake up just one more time.

Initially, forty-four-year-old Mary Applebee did not want to make the trip from Buffalo to Conneaut. For one, she had always had an aversion to traveling by water. For another, she had not been feeling in the best of health of late. However, James, her son, insisted that a trip to Ohio to see some of her favorite relatives would do her spirits good. After some hesitation, Mary agreed, and preparations were made for her to travel from her home in Colden to Buffalo, where she would accompany James on his journey to Conneaut on the schooner *New Connecticut*.

A modern replica of an 1800s wooden schooner, similar to the one that Mary Applebee was on when it wrecked off Portland, New York. *From Wikipedia Commons*.

When she arrived at Buffalo, plans were halted as a fierce summer storm blew across the lake for two straight days. While Mary listened to the storm hammer the shore, her apprehension returned. Fortunately, on the morning of August 14, the lake was smooth as glass, and Mary and the crew embarked on a pleasant journey to Ohio.

For the next three weeks, Mary thoroughly enjoyed time with her relatives, some she had not seen since her childhood. Yet as the days passed and the time of her departure drew near, Mary wrote that "a deep solemnity" descended upon her, depriving her of sleep that last week. As she tossed and turned into the nights, she was reminded of a nightmare that she had dreamt years before. Waking with a shudder the day before her departure, Mary sent word to James that she would return to New York by way of stagecoach.

Yet, perhaps because the schooner would be captained by her nephew and crewed by her son along with several other experienced sailors, Mary was ultimately convinced to return home by way of the water.

On the morning of September 4, the *New Connecticut*, loaded with wheat and flour, set sail. With a good eastern wind from behind, the schooner easily cut across the choppy waters, moving up the estimated time of arrival at Buffalo to 10:00 p.m. that very evening, instead of in the early morning hours of the next day.

As Mary watched the scenery from the deck that morning, she felt some excitement at the prospect of an early return to her husband and home. But even with the thought of not spending the night on the ship, Mary could not completely shed the feeling of dread. As she gazed into the noonday sky, she noted the presence of gathering dark clouds casting their gray shadows onto the water. Was she imagining that the waves were beginning to lift higher and showing off sharp foamy peaks?

Quickly, she turned from her perch as her anxiety, like the waves, grew higher each moment. Searching for comfort, she pulled out the small hymnal she carried with her. As the book fell open in her lap, she noted the first words on the page:

> *Happy soul, thy days are ended, all the mourning day below,*
> *Go by angel guards attended, to the side of Jesus go.*

Over the next half hour, as Mary turned through the hymnal, the wind whipped the pages about, displaying the same hymn three more times.

Around this time, Mary noticed that she could see the village of Erie, Pennsylvania. Comparing the flat stillness of the land to the motion of the lake, she was certain now that the weather was taking a turn for the worse.

With this, she approached several of the sailors, insisting that they needed to take precautions. When the crew assured Mary that they had seen much worse, she became frustrated and went below deck to see the captain, who had taken ill that morning. Here again, her fears were dismissed by the captain, suggesting that the crew would let him know if they were in immediate danger.

As Mary made her way to the top, she resigned herself to the situation. Her fate was and always had been in the hands of God. While meditating on this, she felt a violent shudder throughout the ship as a gale blasted through the sails. Immediately after, the captain appeared on the deck and began shouting orders.

Within minutes, the *New Connecticut* and its crew found themselves in the midst of a full-blown Lake Erie storm. The crew scrambled about as the rain and wind unleashed all its fury onto the small vessel. The captain, yelling inaudibly over the sound, took Mary by the arm and ushered her below deck. Quickly, he shut the companion hatch, only to have it violently fly open again. For an instant, he turned back toward the open door as if to shut and latch it down, but for an unknown reason, he changed his mind and returned to the sails.

Below, Mary began to pray, as she believed it would not be long now before she would meet her maker. While she prayed, though, a sensation came about that she needed to do something more. It was then that she poked her head through the open hatch. Frighteningly, she noted that two sailors were clinging to the railing, calling aloud, their voices carried away in the gale.

As she began to descend, she was met with a scene just as terrifying. She saw the beds falling from their berths. Before she had time to consider this, she was thrown from her position while she felt the entire ship lurch sideways.

Trying to make sense of her surroundings, Mary felt the rush of water bursting from all directions. Scrambling to find her balance, she realized that her dress was caught on something, pinning her to the wall, which had become the new floor when the vessel rolled to its side. Frantically, she tried to kick free while loose furniture began to slam into her body. With waves of water now beginning to cover her face, Mary took what she thought was her last breath.

Miraculously, just as she felt herself surrendering to her death, she somehow found herself floating on top of the water, in a small space about four by two feet. Floating there, listening to the groaning of the ship, Mary contemplated her surroundings, realizing she was most likely above an upper berth. With this knowledge, she lowered herself from her horizontal position where she had been floating and let her legs explore below the water. To her relief, her feet found a stronghold on the bottom berth, allowing her to stand while holding on to the top bunk.

With the rocking of the ship, items brushed up against Mary's legs. She soon found a mattress and a canister of tea, which she positioned on the board below her feet in order to create a makeshift seat. Sitting down, her shoulders barely above water, Mary gave into her exhaustion, sleeping throughout the night, never once waking until daybreak.

Waking with a start, she assessed her surroundings once again. For one, she realized that the continuous pitching of the ship had stopped. Likewise, she noted that the water appeared to be at the same level as the night before. Finally, she could still hear the wind blowing somewhere above, but she was certain it was becoming less furious as the morning wore on.

Throughout the day, she alternated between standing and sitting, never leaving the air supply in her small space. The only break in the monotony came in the afternoon, when Mary thought she heard a steamboat passing by. With the wind still whistling overhead, she realized that it was impossible for anyone on the steamer to hear her cries. For the next several hours, the lone passenger of the *New Connecticut* passed the time by humming hymns and praying.

As darkness descended on her once again, Mary gave thanks as she drifted into a surprisingly restful sleep.

Waking the next morning, she heard what she thought was the crew walking about the vessel and moving around the heavy ropes. She wondered why they were not calling out to her, but she thought perhaps they were so grief-stricken they could not speak. In any case, she found peace that they were aboard and was most thankful when she felt the water level decrease by an inch or so. They must have somehow shifted the vessel using the ropes, giving Mary hope throughout the day that she would soon be rescued.

After another peaceful night of sleep, Mary awoke to agonizing hunger pangs. She realized how weak and exhausted she felt that morning and knew that she needed to find sustenance to revive her strength. Over the course of the morning, as her hunger grew, she allowed herself, for the first time since the storm, to feel the building despair. Why would God allow her to tarry so long in the walls of a sunken ship just to allow her to starve to death?

As she cried there on her perch, however, she suddenly remembered that Jesus had fasted for forty days and nights, while she had gone without food for only three.

After asking God for forgiveness, Mary opened her eyes and gazed about her surroundings. Astonishingly, there, floating on the water, was a cracker and a small pat of butter.

Later that afternoon, she heard footsteps somewhere above her, followed by voices. This time, she used all her strength to call out to the crew, instructing them to throw down a rope. Eventually, a long metal pole poked through the ceiling and stretched into the water, as if it were a spoon stirring soup. Because she could not reach the pole from her station, Mary used a broomstick and began rapping against the pole, but to no avail. Feeling defeated, she watched as the pole was pulled back up through the opening. Shortly after, all sounds from above ended. She was left alone in her confinement once again.

On that fourth night, while sleeping, during her only respite from captivity, she was aware that another storm had arrived. The cabin began rocking from side to side, and she heard the furniture and dishes crashing together and felt the water rising, yet she never awoke enough to fear it.

The next morning, she woke with the realization that she had survived yet another ordeal. As the hours passed into afternoon and then evening, the water continued to rise, finally stopping at neck level. This, in turn, forced her back to a standing position in order to keep her head above the cold water. Incredibly, she was able to sleep through the night without ever letting go from her perch.

On her fifth morning, Mary noted the weakened condition of her state. After standing in deep water, having very little food and losing hope, she began to accept that her chance of survival was very slim. Struggling throughout the day, Mary prayed for strength and courage in whatever was to come. As she fell in and out of consciousness, she was vaguely aware of the footsteps above. However, not able to reason clearly, Mary allowed herself to slip back into the relief of sleep.

Somewhere in the darkness, though, Mary realized that her surroundings were now shifting. Half awake and still half asleep, she contemplated the feeling. It was difficult to distinguish reality from dream. Yet when she felt a sharp jerking motion, she used all her mental energy to come to. Fully awake now, she realized that something was happening. The entire vessel was moving. Voices were overhead. Quickly gathering all her strength, Mary reached for the broom and began to bang on the side. After a few minutes, she concluded that no one could hear her, but she continued to make a racket regardless.

After a while, the vessel seemed to slow and then stop. Mary considered that the ship had most likely been towed to the nearest harbor. Still hearing the voices and footsteps above, she realized that this could be her last chance to survive, as she was certain she could not endure another night in her condition.

With a quick prayer, Mary let go from her position and began to swim for it. Just as someone opened the companionway door, Mary pushed through the opening. As she blinked into the brightness of the sun, she quickly made out the shape of two figures standing over her. Although she could not clearly see, she heard the voice of her nephew and the cry of her son.

As Mary began to sit up, a collective gasp was heard as a crowd had grown around her. For the sailors as well as her nephew and son believed they had just found her drowned body. When they realized she was attempting to stand up, one sailor yelled to "come see the dead woman walking." Silently, though, a great realization moved over the crowd. They were not looking at a ghost or the living dead. Instead, they were gazing upon a real-life miracle. For Mary had survived underwater for five days.

Quickly, Mary was loaded onto a nearby vessel. Although in a very weakened state, Mary inquired of her whereabouts. Believing she was near Conneaut, she was surprised to learn that the ship had crashed on the rocks near Portland Harbor in New York, not far from its designated port.

For the next four days, Mary recovered at an inn in Portland. There was an outpouring of kindness as people learned of her frightening ordeal. Likewise, newspapers across the country picked up the story and told of her miraculous survival.

As Mary began to heal, she was able to piece the story together. She learned that all sailors on board had made it safely to the lifeboat. Several attempts were made to rescue Mary before leaving the scene, but hope was lost when most of the vessel sank. Likewise, on the second day, Mary learned that some of the crew returned to look for her. They stuck a pole into the cabin hoping to hook her body. Finally, Mary learned that on the day of her rescue, the crew was making one last attempt to recover her body. Her funeral was scheduled for that afternoon, and they had hoped to retrieve her body for a proper burial.

Years later, Mary wrote of her time spent in the bowels of the schooner. She wrote the following:

> I shall always retain feelings of strong gratitude for Doctors Bradley, Fisk and Gale for their humane attentions to me, and professional services while at Portland, for which they declined receiving an remuneration. Also, the kindness and human assistance I received from my friends

and other individuals, has made a deep and lasting impression on my mind; but the feeling of gratitude and love are more especially awakened towards that Being who rules the universe, and who merciful providence was so wonderfully exercised in preserving me, and rescuing me from the very jaws of death.

BIBLIOGRAPHY

Books and Articles

Angstadt, Jeremy. "Killers on Kelleys Island: The 1911 Triple Murder on the Island." YouTube. December 27, 2019. Accessed April 9, 2021. https://www.youtube.com.

Applebee, Mary. *A Narrative of the Wreck of the Schooner New Connecticut, on Lake Erie, Sept. 4, 1833: Together with an Account of the Miraculous Preservation of Mrs. Mary Applebee, Who Was Confined in the Cabin Five Days! The Schooner Being for the Greater Part of the Time, Immersed in Water!* Buffalo, NY: H.A. Salisbury, 1834.

Boyer, Dwight. *Strange Adventures of the Great Lakes.* New York: Dodd, Mead, 1974.

Buhk, Tobin T. "The Last Pirate: Joseph Kerwin, the Erie Strangler (1904)." Accessed April 9, 2021. http://www.darkcornersofhistory.com.

Caldwell, Mitchell. "The Prostitution of Lying in Wait." *University of Miami Law Review* 57, no. 2 (March 1, 2003). Accessed April 9, 2021. https://repository.law.miami.edu.

Dark Histories Podcast. "The Curious Case of Not Townsend." Accessed April 9, 2021. https://www.darkhistories.com.

Erie Reader. "Not Gone, Not Forgotten." Accessed April 9, 2021. https://www.eriereader.com.

Find a Grave. "Millions of Cemetery Records." Accessed April 9, 2021. https://www.findagrave.com.

Fraser, Chad. *Lake Erie Stories: Struggle and Survival on a Freshwater Ocean.* Toronto, ON: Dundurn Press, 2017.

Gault, Robert H., S. Ferenczi and Ernest Jones. "Contributions to Psycho-Analysis." *Journal of the American Institute of Criminal Law and Criminology* 9, no. 2 (1918): 313. doi:10.2307/1133853.

Grainger, Jennifer. *Vanished Villages of Elgin.* Toronto: Natural Heritage Books, 2008.

Hebert, Lou. *Hidden History of Toledo.* Charleston, SC: The History Press, 2019.

History by Zim. "Mug Shots: Joseph Kerwin." July 22, 2019. Accessed April 9, 2021. http://www.historybyzim.com.

Klein, Christopher. "The Battle of Lake Erie, 200 Years Ago." History.com. September 10, 2013. Accessed April 9, 2021. https://www.history.com.

Millender, Sarah. *History Of Pontiac Correctional Center: A Bibliography Of Sources Available at the Pontiac Public Library.* IL: Prison Public Memory Project, 2017.

Murray, John Wilson. *Memoirs of a Great Detective: Incidents in the Life of John Wilson Murray.* Place of Publication Not Identified: Nabu Press, 2010.

Myers, Bill. "Toledo History Box." Toledo History Box. March 29, 2012. Accessed April 9, 2021. https://www.toledohistorybox.com.

Norway Heritage. "Disaster on Lake Erie in 1852." Accessed April 9, 2021. http://www.norwayheritage.com.

Popular Pittsburgh. "Italian Heritage." April 9, 2020. Accessed April 9, 2021. https://popularpittsburgh.com.

Reports of Cases Argued and Determined in the Ohio Circuit Courts: Ohio Circuit Decisions. Norwalk, OH: Laning Printing Company. Accessed April 9, 2021. https://books.google.com.

Stiger, John, ed. *Recidivism among Criminal Offenders: A Review of the Literature.* Washington State Department of Health and Human Services, 1986. opj.gov.

Vermilion Views. "The Tailor's Son." Accessed April 9, 2021. http://www.vermilionohio.org.

Wallace, W. Stewart. "The Townsend Case: Maclean's: April 15th 1931." Maclean's, the Complete Archive. Accessed April 9, 2021. https://archive.macleans.ca.

Wright, Larry, and Patricia Wright. *Great Lakes Lighthouses Encyclopedia.* Richmond Hill, Ont.: Boston Mills Press, 2011.

BIBLIOGRAPHY

Newspapers

Ashtabula Star Beacon
Buffalo Daily
Buffalo Enquirer
Cleveland Plain Dealer
Denver Post
Detroit Free Press
Sandusky Register
Toledo News Bee

ABOUT THE AUTHOR

Wendy Koile is the Director of Teaching and Learning and a part-time English instructor at Central Ohio Technical College. She holds a master's degree in teaching as well as a newly earned master's in the art of English. Wendy has been an avid Lake Erie lover her entire life and continues to visit and research the area to this day. This is her fourth book with The History Press.